NINJA FOODI C
WITH LATEST RE
2021

270 DELICIOUS RECIPES WHICH SAVES YOU TIME WHILE IMPRESSING YOUR LOVED ONES

WRITTEN BY COLLIE MORGAN

© **Copyright 2021.**

All rights reserved.

It is not legal to copy or reproduce any of the content in this book by printed or digital format without author's permission. Screen recording or any sort of other recordings are not allowed as well. This book has been created for personal use only. You are not allowed to sell, share, rent, issue or quote any sort of content from this book. The book is protected by copyrights.

Disclaimer Note

This book has been written to educate and share knowledge. Publisher is not committed or guaranteed that all the tips and suggestions will become successful for each and every person. Publisher and the author of this book is not responsible for any losses or damages caused by the content of this book directly or indirectly.

TABLE OF CONTENTS

INTRODUCTION 1

CHAPTER 1 – WHAT IS NINJA FOODI? 4
    1.1 DIFFERENT MODELS OF NINJA FOODI MULTI COOKERS 5
    1.2 MAIN FUNCTIONALITIES OF NINJA FOODI MULTI COOKER 6
    1.3 WHAT ARE THE MAIN USES OF NINJA FOODI MULTI COOKER? 6
    1.4 WHAT YOU GET WITH THE NINJA FOODI AND IT'S SETUP GUIDE 7
    1.5 GET TO KNOW THE CONTROLS OF THE NINJA FOODI 8

CHAPTER 2 – ADVANTAGES OF NINJA FOODI MULTI COOKER 13

CHAPTER 3 – HOW TO PROPERLY USE YOUR NINJA FOODI MULTICOOKER? 17
    3.1 HOW EACH LID IS USED? 17
    3.2 ALL IN ONE POT COOKING 19
    3.3 QUICK PRESSURE RELEASE VS NATURAL PRESSURE RELEASE 20
    3.4 CAN YOU COOK REGULAR MEALS IN THE NINJA FOODI? 21

CHAPTER 4 – HOW TO CLEAN & MAINTAIN YOUR NINJA FOODI MULTI COOKER 22
    4.1 THE PROPER WAY TO CLEAN YOUR NINJA FOODI 22
    4.2 HOW TO STORE YOUR NINJA FOODI? 25

CHAPTER 5 – TECHNOLOGY RELATED WITH NINJA FOODI MULTI COOKER 26
    5.1 HOW TECHNOLOGY HAS BEEN USED IN NINJA FOODI? 26
    5.2 WHAT IS TENDER CRISP TECHNOLOGY AND HOW TO USE IT? 27
    5.3 HOW TO PERFECTLY TENDERCRISP? 28

5.4 GENERAL TIPS ABOUT THE NINJA FOODI 29

CHAPTER 6 – COMMON MISTAKES AND HOW TO AVOID THEM 31

CHAPTER 7 – BREAKFAST RECIPES 32

1. APPLE DUMPLINGS 32
2. AIR FRIED FISH MUFFINS 34
3. AIR FRIED CHEESE BREAD 36
4. AIR FRIED GARLIC BREAD 38
5. APPLE MIXED FLAT BREAD 40
6. AIR FRIED FISH ROLLS 42
7. BATTER FRIED FISH 44
8. CRUNCHY BACON SLICES 46
9. CORN ZUCCHINI ROTI 47
10. CHICKEN PATTIES 50
11. CHEESY HAM SANDWICH WITH HOT SAUCE 52
12. CLASSIC BREAKFAST 54
13. DELICIOUS FILLED PEPPERS 56
14. ENERGETIC CHICKEN NOODLE THICK SOUP 58
15. FRIED BROWN BREAD STICKS 60
16. FRIED SALMON 62
17. FRIED CHEESE TOAST 64
18. HOME FRIES 66
19. HOMEMADE SWEET POTATO BITES 68
20. HOT DOGS WITH MELTED CHEESE 70
21. HEALTHY MORNING CASSEROLE 72
22. HOT CHICKEN & VEGE BITES 74
23. KETOGENIC EGG MUFFIN 75
24. LOW STARCH FRIED EGG BITES 77
25. MAYO BURGER 78

26. NUTRITIOUS MORNING PUFF 80

27. NINJA FRIED POTATOES 82

28. PRESSURE COOKED RICE 84

29. PORK TACOS 86

30. STIR FRIED BEANS 89

31. STANDARD BREAKFAST 90

32. SMOOTH FRITTATA 92

33. STIR FRIED SAUSAGES WITH MASHED POTATOES 94

34. STEAMED TENDER CHICKEN BUN 96

35. STRACHY LOW CARB SOUP 98

36. SWEET POTATO SQUASH 100

37. STEAMED OATS WITH BROWN SUGAR SYRUP 102

38. SPICY POTATOES WITH FRIED EGGS 104

39. SIMPLE RISOTTO 106

40. STEAK SUBMARINE 108

41. SPICY CHICKEN SALAD WITH CRISPY TORTILLAS 110

42. SHREDDED CHICKEN WITH STEAMED RICE 112

43. TINY APPLE BITES 114

44. TENDER CRISPED BURGER 116

45. TUNA CAKES 117

46. TENDER CRISPED CHICKPEAS 119

47. TASTY POTATO SLICES WITH SOUR CREAM 121

48. TWISTED BREAD MIX 123

49. TENDER BEANS WITH MELTED DRESSING 124

50. TENDER CRISPED CORN 126

CHAPTER 8 – LUNCH RECIPES 128

1. ALL IN ONE SPECIAL CHICKEN 128

2. ASPARAGUS WITH WRAPPED BACONS 130

3. BOILED EGGS 132

4. BEEF STEW 133

5. BELL PEPPER SAUSAGE SALAD 135

6. CHICKEN FRIED RICE 136

7. CREAMY CHEESE SHRIMP CURRY 138

8. EGG FRIED RICE..140

9. CRISPY PIE 142

10. CREAMY SPAGHETTI 144

11. CHILI DRUMSTICKS 146

12. CHICKEN WITH CRISPY NACHOS..148

13. KAN KUN CHICKEN SALAD 150

14. CHICKEN POT CURRY AND RICE 151

15. CHEESY MACARONI 153

16. CHICKEN SOUP...155

17. CUBED POTATO FRIES..157

18. CABBAGE BACON CASSEROLE 159

19. FRIED RICE & PORK 160

20. FRIED PORK CHOPS 162

21. FRIED HERB CHICKEN..164

22. FRIED PRAWNS WITH DICED VEGGIES 166

23. FRIED VEGETABLES WITH SLICED BEEF 167

24. HOT AND SWEET CHICKEN WITH BRUSSELS SPROUTS...................169

25. HOT PEPPER BEEF 171

26. HOME MADE MEATBALLS 173

27. MEATLOAF & STEAMED VEGETABLES 175

28. NUTRITIOUS BEAN CASSEROLE 177

29. PASTA WITH BEEF..179

30. PORK POTATO TWIST 181

31. CHICKEN & SWEET POTATOES...183

32. PRESSURE COOKED SPINACH WITH SLICED PUMPKINS 184

33. PORK MACARONI 186

34. PRESSURE COOKED TURKEY WITH NOODLES 188

35. ROASTED BEEF & POTATO 190

36. ROAST CHICKEN BITES 192

37. SLICED POTATOES WITH ROASTED BEEF 193

38. SPAGETTI AND FRIED RIBS 195

39. SIMPLE RICE DIET 196

40. SWEET CHICKEN WING RICE 197

41. SAUSAGE VEGETABLE MIX 199

42. STEAMED PORK 200

43. SPICY BEEF MIX 201

44. SWEET POTATO CHICKEN DISH 203

45. STEAMED CHICKEN TORTILLAS 204

46. SHRIMP RICE 206

47. STEAK & BROCCOLI MIX 208

48. VEGETABLE NOODLES 210

49. VEGGIE & CHICKEN KABOBS 212

50. ZUCCHINI CUP CAKES 214

CHAPTER 9 – DINNER RECIPES 215

1. AIR FRIED PIZZA 215

2. AIR FRIED SHRIMPS 218

3. AIR FRIED PASTA COMBO 219

4. AIR FRIED CHICKEN WRAPPERS 220

5. AIR FRIED POTATO CUBES 222

6. BEEF KEBOBS 223

7. BAKED CHEESE PASTA 224

8. CHICKEN SOUP WITH BEANS AND CORN 226

9. CHEESY MACARONI 228

10. CANNED BEEF WITH SHREDDED CABBAGE 230

11. CAULI FLOWER SOUP 232
12. CHICKEN & BACON FILLED JALAPENOS 234
13. CHICKEN STEW 235
14. CREAMY FISH 237
15. CHEESY MACARONI & BACON 239
16. FRIED FISH WITH VEGETABLE SALAD 241
17. FISH LASAGNA 242
18. FRIED ZUCCHINI 244
19. FRIED SPICY CHICKEN KABOBS 246
20. GREEN ONION SOUP 248
21. HOMEMADE YOGURT 250
22. HOT CHICKEN WRAPPER 251
23. HOT SPAGETTI & BEEF 253
24. KETOGENIC CHICKEN SOUP 255
25. LOW CARB HEALTHY PASTA 256
26. LIME MIXED TUNA SLICES 258
27. MIXED VEGETABLE BROTH 260
28. MIXED CHEESE SOUP 263
29. MIXED SEAFOOD NOODLE FIESTA 265
30. NUTRITIOUS BEEF STEW 267
31. PRESSURE COOKED SAUSAGE PASTA MIX 269
32. PRESSURE COOKED RICE WITH FRIED CHICKEN 271
33. POTATO BROTH 273
34. PORK TACOS 275
35. PRESSURE COOKED DEVILLED CHICKEN 277
36. QUICK CHEESY BEEF SOUP 279
37. RICE AND BEEF PECCADILLO 281
38. ROASTED BEEF WITH SLICED CARROTS 283
39. RED CABBAGE SOUP 285

- 40. SAUSAGE CHEESE LASAGNA ... 287
- 41. SPICY BEEF STEW ... 289
- 42. STIR FRIED CARROTS ... 291
- 43. STEAMED BEANS WITH MASHED POTATOES ... 293
- 44. SMOOTH LASAGNA ... 294
- 45. SLICED BEEF WITH CHIPS ... 296
- 46. SIMPLE DHAL SOUP ... 298
- 47. SAUSAGE MIXED CORN SOUP ... 300
- 48. TURKEY WITH GRREN BEANS ... 301
- 49. TURKEY STOCK ... 302
- 50. TENDER CRISPED TURKEY ... 304

CHAPTER 10 – DESSERT RECIPES ... 306

- 1. AIR FRIED FRITTERS ... 306
- 2. AIR FRIED PEACHES ... 308
- 3. AIR FRIED SWEET PATTIES ... 310
- 4. BAKED APPLES ... 312
- 5. CHERRY PIE ... 313
- 6. COCONUT CREAM CAKE ... 315
- 7. COCOA MIXED STRAWBERRIES ... 318
- 8. CHOCOLATE CUPCAKES ... 320
- 9. CEREAL FILLED BANANAS ... 322
- 10. CHOCOLATE LAVA CUBES ... 323
- 11. CHOCO MIXED ZUCCHINI BREAD ... 324
- 12. DANISH CREAM CHEESE WITH RED CHERRIES ... 326
- 13. FRUITY DUMPLINGS ... 327
- 14. FRIED EGG ROLLS WITH CHOPPED APPLES ... 328
- 15. FRIED S'MORES ... 330
- 16. FRENCH TOAST ... 331
- 17. FRIED APPLE FRIES ... 332

18. HEALTHY BREAD PUDDING 334

19. LOW CARB CHEESE CAKE 336

20. LOW SUGAR CHOCOLATE CAKE 338

21. LOW SUGAR BROWNIES 340

22. LEMON FLAVORED CHEESE CAKE 342

23. LOW CARB CHOCOLATE DONUTS 344

24. MIXED FOOD CAKE 346

25. OATS WITH CHOPPED APPLES 347

26. PUMPKIN PIE 349

27. REFRESHING BANANA CAKE 350

28. SLICED BANANA WITH PEANUT BUTTER 352

29. SWEET BERRY TARTS 353

30. SLICED BANANA WITH MIXED NUTS 354

CHAPTER 11 – VEGETARIAN RECIPES 356

1. AIR FRIED CORN 356

2. AIR FRIED SPICY TOFU 357

3. BAKED LINED POTATOES 359

4. BATTERED CUCUMBER FRIES 361

5. CRUNCHY SLICED POTATOES 362

6. CARROT FRIES 363

7. CHEESY BEAN FRIES 364

8. CRISPY SPROUTS 365

9. CABBAGE WEDGES 366

10. CRISPY CAULI FLOWERS 368

11. CUCUMBER PASTA MIX 369

12. EASY VEGETABLE SOUP 371

13. FRIED EGGPLANT SLICES 373

14. FRIED SLICED BEETS 375

15. FRIED KALE CHIPS 377

- 16. FRIED ZUCCHINI SLICES 378
- 17. FRIED VEGGIES WITH BALANCED NUTRITIONS 380
- 18. FRIED SLICED PUMPKIN 381
- 19. HEALTHY ASPARAGUS BITES 382
- 20. PICKLE FRIES 383
- 21. POTATO BEAN TWISTER 384
- 22. PANKO COATED OKRA 386
- 23. ROASTED THIN POTATOES 387
- 24. STEAMED CHOY SALAD 389
- 25. SPICY SWEET POTATOES 391
- 26. SPINACH POTATO TWIST 392
- 27. SEASONED FRIED MUSHROOMS 394
- 28. SWEET FRIED APPLE CHIPS 396
- 29. SPROUT BITES 397
- 30. VEGETABLE FRIED RICE 398

CHAPTER 12 – SEAFOOD RECIPES 400

- 1. AIR FRIED COD 400
- 2. AIR FRIED TUNA FILLETS 402
- 3. AIR FRIED SHRIMPS 403
- 4. CRUNCHY TUNA SLICES 404
- 5. CHEESY SHRIMP & TOMATO MIX 406
- 6. COCONUT MIXED TUNA CURRY 408
- 7. CHEESE ADDED PRAWN SALAD 410
- 8. FRIED SHRIMP RICE 413
- 9. FRIED BATTERED SHRIMPS 415
- 10. GRILLED PRAWNS 417
- 11. GARLIC PRAWNS 418
- 12. HOT SALTY FRIED FISH 419
- 13. LOBSTER SOUP 421

14. LEMON FLAVORED TUNA BITES 423

15. MIX SALMON STEW 425

16. PRAWN NOODLES...427

17. PRESSURE COOKED SALMON 429

18. PEPPER SPICED SHRIMP RICE 431

19. PRESSURE COOKED CRAB LEGS 433

20. TILAPIA TACOS 434

21. SEASONED LOBSTER 436

22. SIMPLY FRIED PRAWNS 438

23. STEMED CRABS..440

24. STEAMED FISH & POTATOES 442

25. STEAMED PRAWNS WITH CARROTS...444

26. SHRIMP & MACARONI 446

27. TUNA NOODLE SOUP 448

28. SPICY SALMON...449

29. SEAFOOD SOUP 451

30. SALMON CAKES 452

CHAPTER 13 – MEAT & POULTRY RECIPES 454

1. AIR FRIED RIBS 454

2. AIR FRYED CHICKEN 455

3. AIR FRIED BEEF LOAF 457

4. AIR FRIED BEEF SLICES 458

5. AIR FRYED TURKEY BREAST 460

6. PRESSURE COOKED DEVILLED CHICKEN 462

7. BEEF CUBES...463

8. BATTER FRIED CHICKEN CRISPIES 465

9. BEEF RIBS WITH MAPLE SYRUP 467

10. CRISPY CHICKEN WINGS 469

11. CHEESY CRISPY WINGS 471

12. CINNAMON PORK SLICES 472
13. CHICKEN BALLLS 474
14. CHEESE MIXED CHICKEN BREAST 476
15. CHICKEN KABOBS 477
16. CHEESE MIXED GARLIC CHICKEN 479
17. FRIED CHICKEN WINGS 481
18. FRIED PRESSURE COOKED PORK 482
19. GARLIC SEASONED PORK 484
20. HAM & PEACH ROAST 486
21. HOT & SPICY NUGGETS 487
22. PORK CHOPS & SOUR CREAM 488
23. PRESSURE COOKED BACK RIBS 489
24. PORK TORTILLAS 491
25. PORK SALSA 493
26. ROASTED BRISKET 494
27. STUFFED CHICKEN 495
28. SPICY FRIED HAM 497
29. SWEET FRIED CHICKEN 499
30. TENDER CHICKEN FRIES 501

CONCLUSION 503

INTRODUCTION

People used to prepare their meals even before the stone age. Which means they did some modifications to the food before consuming. Such like cleaning, frying, and drying. With the time humankind began to discover new methods as well as equipments to prepare their meals. In early ages they used sharp stones to tear meat and slice vegetables. Then they used clay pots and containers to store and cook meals. So after thousands of years we have come to this stage. Now as a species we have discovered so many new meal preparation techniques and methods. Because of them our life style has become easier than ever before. When talking about equipments, multi cookers are one of them.

This product is relatively new when comparing to other cooking appliances we use in our kitchen. Yes the basic multi cookers were invented few decades ago. But this new multi-purpose multi cookers came to the market within a decade. Ninja foodi multi cooker is a product like that. You can do various types of cooking using this multi cooker. Such like air frying, pressure cooking, slow cooking and many other things. In this book you will discover everything you need to know regarding the ninja foodi multi cooker. Until now ninja foodi has released two types of multi cookers. They are "Ninja Foodi Original" and "Ninja Foodi Deluxe". In this book you will be able to know each and every small detail regarding both of these models. You might be having a ninja foodi multi cooker by now or else you might be a new user. Doesn't matter your present situation. In the first chapter you can get all the proper instructions and guidelines regarding setting up and using this equipment. The author has gone to the simplest detail to give a proper idea to the reader. For an example, all the controls and the parts have been described in detail for both models. So by referring this book, even a brand new user will be able use this equipment without any issue. Sometimes a person might think why I should use a ninja foodi multi cooker. There is a list of answers for that question in the second chapter.

We can see so many kitchen appliances in the present market. But think for a moment how many of them are being used properly, under the manufacture guide lines? You know the answer. The main reason for that is lack of knowledge. So the whole chapter three has been targeted on the tips you should follow when using the ninja foodi multi cooker. The next chapter is equally important as the previous chapter. Because maintaining and cleaning has a direct link to proper usage. So all the things you should know regarding cleaning and maintaining have been included in forth chapter.

Most users are curious about the technical background of the appliance. In this multi cooker, you will find a combination of several simple technologies. As a result of that combination you will be surprised with the results of this product. For more have look at the fifth chapter. Most of the time people talk about the things they shouldn't do. Sadly when it comes to the real life scenario, those points aren't coming to their minds. To minimize that, we have created a list which we have found from a thorough research related with multi cooker users. So you can get to know that list in sixth chapter. Therefore you will be able to avoid them as well.

From the seventh chapter you can experience the recipes that you can try with your ninja foodi multi cooker. There are hundreds of recipes under seven categories in this book. They have been categorized as breakfast, lunch, dinner, desserts, vegetarian, fish & seafood and meat & poultry recipes. You will be able to try almost every cooking functionality which comes with the ninja foodi multi cooker from these recipes. Apart from that you will be able prepare some healthy and delicious meals from these recipes.

CHAPTER 1

WHAT IS NINJA FOODI?

When it comes to meal preparation, frying and boiling can be considered as the basics methods people used to follow. With the time and advancement of technology the same principles have been further developed. Today we can see various types of kitchen appliances designed for different purposes. Oven, Air fryer, Pressure cooker, Hot plate, Toaster are some of them. There is one common factor for each and every one of these appliance. That is they have been designed to do one certain task. But with the time people wanted all in one products, which could do multiple tasks while saving time. As a result of that several products were invented. Multi cooker was one of them.

Would you believe if someone says the history of multi cookers will go back to 1920's? Don't be surprised with that. Because that is true. The first multi cooker was invented in that era in England. Those models weren't complex as modern multi cookers. They were so simple and the main intention was to reduce the gas usage and save money. With the time several other countries tried to invent newer versions of multi cookers. In 1936 America invented another multi cooker concept with slow cooking technology. In 1950's Japan presented their products to the market.

So by decade after decade several new functionalities were added to this product. So at the present moment multi cookers have become way more advanced than ever before. They are equipped with temperature controls, pressure controls and built in timer. These options will definitely help consumer to gain a maximum efficiency with the product. Not only that, but also the range of food types you can cook in your multi cooker have developed throughout these years. You can try grains, soups and broths, meat & poultry, vegetables and fish & seafood in a modern multi cooker. As a plus you will be able try them under several cuisines.

So as per the name of this chapter you can understand "what is Ninja Foodi". It is a multi-cooker with cutting edge technology. You can use it to prepare your daily meals. In next sections you will be able to discover the other things related with Ninja Foodi multi cooker.

1.1 DIFFERENT MODELS OF NINJA FOODI MULTI COOKERS

Currently there are two main Ninja Foodi multi cooker models. One is called Ninja Foodi Original and the other one is called Ninja Foodi Deluxe. Both of these cookers have almost the same functionalities. The difference comes with the generations. Ninja Foodi Original is the senior member of these two products. It was founded in mid of 2018. The Ninja Foodi Deluxe was founded in 2019. That has a new interface and few added functionalities than the Original Ninja Foodi multi cooker. You can purchase both of these models in current market. The newer "Deluxe model" is bit more expensive than the "Original model".

1.2 MAIN FUNCTIONALITIES OF NINJA FOODI MULTI COOKER

There are several types of multi cookers. Almost every multi cooker has been designed to do variety of tasks. Ninja Foodi multi cooker has been designed to accomplish two main objectives. That is to air frying and pressure cooking food. Other than that there are several things you can do with this product. It can slow cook, saute and grill your dishes as well. The item has all the options which are required to do all the tasks.

You can prepare dishes using this product on individual requirement basis. Such as just for air fry or pressure cook. Or you can use multiple functions on your desired dish. Tender crisp technology is something comes with this Ninja Foodi multi cooker which is relevant to above mentioned fact. In future chapters you will discover those technologies and methods.

1.3 WHAT ARE THE MAIN USES OF NINJA FOODI MULTI COOKER?

As mentioned in the previous section, there are number of things you can get done with this product. Most of the time people use this to pressure cooking and air frying purposes.

Due to its large size it can cook large amount of food at once. When using the air fryer function it is almost like a regular air fryer. Most of the time it uses the built in oils and liquids to cook the food. Sometimes you will have to add some amount of oil and water in order to reach the desired result. But when it comes to the pressure cooking function it is not the same. You will have to stick in to the basics and must follow regular pressure cooking standards.

In here I will give a simple introduction to the tender crisped cooking. It may sound so strange but it is not that complicated to do so. By now you know that Ninja Foodi multi cooker is equipped with two main functions. They are air frying and pressure cooking. So for an example you can pressure cook a chicken. After that it will become tender. Then you can remove the pressure cooking lid and turn on the air fry function. Then it will become crispier. As you expected that defines the tender crisp technology.

1.4 WHAT YOU GET WITH THE NINJA FOODI AND IT'S SETUP GUIDE

What is in the box of "Ninja Foodi Original" Multi Cooker?

In this section I will be explaining both types of ninja foodi multi cookers. First let's consider about the **Ninja Foodi Original Multi Cooker**. This is the senior member of the line. Let's see what you can have in the box.

1. You will get the Ninja Foodi multi cooker with fixed air frying lid.
2. The pressure cooker lid
3. Basket
4. Cooking pot with nonstick ceramic coating
5. Stainless steel rack

Make sure you check the box for all of these things.

What is in the box of "Ninja Foodi Deluxe" Multi Cooker?

With the new "Ninja Foodi Deluxe" you are getting almost the same accessories which you can have with the "Ninja Foodi Original". The only difference is that you will be getting an extra rack to do place your food. Other than that there are no any special parts in the box.

1.5 GET TO KNOW THE CONTROLS OF THE NINJA FOODI

Controls of the Ninja Foodi Original

When it comes to the controls of the **Ninja Foodi Original** you can observe these things. I will start from the left side.

a) Temperature controls
b) Timer controls
c) Just below those buttons you can see functionality buttons such as **pressure, steam, slow cook** and **sauté.**

d) In the next row you can see the controls related with the "tendercrisp" functionality.
e) You can see **air crisp / air fry, bake/roast** and **broil** functions in there.
f) In the right side corner just below the sauté button you can see the button for **dehydration**.
g) In the bottom row **keep warm, start/stop** and **power button** is included.

I have explained that ninja foodi multi cooker has specifically made to do two main tasks. They are air frying and pressure cooking. So when it comes to air frying there are no any special things that you need to follow. Just use it as a regular air fryer.

i. You need to take the basket and place the food item you want to air fry. If you have multiple layers to air fry you can use the rack as well.
ii. Then select the "air crisp" / "air fry" mode and adjust the temperature and frying time.
iii. Close the air frying lid. The fixed lid. (Not the detachable lid)
iv. Then press on start button.

But make sure you use the right lid. The fixed lid has been designed for air frying. So you have to use only that lid. Don't forget to remove the pressure cooking lid before doing that. So apply some cooking spray or small amount of oil to the food item and cook according to the given instructions in the recipe.

When it comes to the pressure cooking it could be something new to lot of you. Keep in your mind that this is not a standard pressure cooker. This is a pressure cooker which works with electricity. Comparing to standard pressure cookers these cookers are quite safe. Still a mistake could lead to an accident.

For this you have to use the cooking pot. You must put some liquid solution to the pot before cooking. It could be water or liquid seasoning mixture. You do not have to fill the cooking pot with that (in future chapters more details will be given). Then place the basket inside the cooking pot. Then put the food item on the basket.

Take the pressure cooker lid and close it. Make sure it closes properly. Also don't forget to check the pressure valve. It must be sealed. Otherwise the pressure will be released.

i. Then turn on the multi cooker by pressing the **power button**.
ii. Then press the **pressure button**.
iii. You can change the pressure levels as well as the cooking time from the top right controllers.
iv. **Once the cooking is done don't just open the pressure lid. It is not safe to do something like that**

(If it is urgent do a quick pressure release. check chapter 3 for more information).

v. Give it 1-5 minutes to settle and release the pressure valve and wait until all the pressure leaves the cooker. (Don't stay too close to the pressure valve. Also make sure nobody is around the equipment when you release the pressure.)

vi. After that the cooker has been depressurized, you can then safely open the lid and take out the cooked food.

Controls of the Ninja Foodi Deluxe

This is an interesting section. Because in new "Ninja Foodi Deluxe" the control panel is completely different than the old one. You will be getting a **center knob to choose the functionalities**.

I will start from the left.

You can see,

- a) **Pressure**
- b) **Steam**
- c) **Slow cook**
- d) **Sauté**

From the right side you can see,

- e) **Air crisp / Air fry**
- f) **Broil**
- g) **Bake/ Roast**

h) **Dehydrate**

The knob itself is the Start/Stop button.

Below that you can see **Temperature** and **Time** controllers.

In the bottom row the **Keep warm** & **Power button** have been placed.

So by rotating the knob you will be able to select the functionality you want to use. After that by pressing **temperature** and **time** buttons you set the required conditions.

The basics for air frying and pressure cooking are same for both of these Ninja Foodi Multi Cookers. Tendercrisp function also has not been changed between these two models. In chapter six you can discover so many things related to tendercrisp technology.

If we do a small comparison between these two "Ninja Foodi Multi Cookers", we can observe small changes with their appearance. The "Ninja Foodi Original" is bit more wider than the new "Ninja Foodi Deluxe". The new model is a bit taller than the old model as well. But those are minor changes. Still you have the freedom to choose product you want. Anyways this book has been written for both Ninja Foodi Original and Ninja Foodi Deluxe users.

CHAPTER 2

ADVANTAGES OF NINJA FOODI MULTI COOKER

There are number of advantages you can have from this appliance. They have been categorized based on their functionality. So let's get to know them.

1. All in One Facility

This is the most important advantage we can have form this product. Which is the combination of two main kitchen appliances together. This multi cooker has been made by combining air fryer and the pressure cooker. Which can save your product cost as well as maintenance cost.

2. Less Smoke

This product doesn't produce much smoke as other kitchen appliances even though it is a combination of two products. The main reason for that is the sealed environment. When pressure cooking, it doesn't release pressure time to time like traditional pressure cookers. Also when it comes to the air fryer it doesn't release much smoke except for the heat which is being released through the air outlet.

3. Multifunction Facility

This product is capable of doing several things other than the air frying and pressure cooking. You can try slow cooking as well as grill / broil functions as well. The manufactures of Ninja Foodi multi cooker has managed to introduce new technologies such as "tendercrisp technology" to the market.

4. Hassel free Cleaning & Operating Ability

Even though this product comes to the market as a multi cooker, the setup structure and the removability is quite simple. As a result of that it is really easy to clean this item. Not only that but also the user friendly interface is really helpful when using this product.

5. Automatic Process

Once after you choose the process and set the temperature and timer that is it. It will be cooked automatically. When it is done the machine notifies you. But it is important to stay closer to the appliance when it is operating. Not only for this product, you should do it for all the electric products. I think you got my point.

6. You will be able to Plan the Meal Preparation Time

This equipment is not like other equipments you use in your kitchen. For each and every function you do with this, will give you an accurate time frame. So you won't waste any time at the first place. Because you can choose the right dish according to the time. As a result of that you can invest more time in other daily tasks in your life.

7. It helps you to Consume Healthy Foods

This product is famous for the less oil consumption as well as for not over cooking the food. So both of these qualities will improve the nutritional and healthy value of the food. Based on the dish you want to prepare, you can choose the oil level in your food. Sometimes you can cook the food with the inbuilt oils and sometimes you can separately add very low amount of oil to gain some extra crispiness to your dish.

8. The Multi Functionality will Save the Energy as well

Did you know that all in one cookers consume less energy than traditional cookers? Surprisingly it is true. Especially Ninja Foodi Multi Cooker doesn't consume much energy. The main benefit of this is the amount of work load it does for the power it consumes. The ratio is quite remarkable. This will definitely help you to manage your power consumption.

9. Safety

This product is a multifunctional cooker but the manufactures have thought a lot about the safety standards of the equipment. Most of you might have used an air fryer at some point in your life. So you know it is generally safe comparing to traditional cooking methods. Same thing goes with this equipments air frying function. When it comes to the pressure cooking function it is a total revolutionized concept. It doesn't release any pressure to the outside while cooking like a traditional pressure cooker. Also the lid is sealed throughout the cooking process. At the end of the cooking you can release all the pressure at once. We recommend to use a long stick to do this process for additional safety. Also don't forget to wear a pair of heat resistant gloves when handling the cooker.

10. Required Less Space

When comparing to its functionalities the total work load it does is amazing. As an additional plus point it does consume a small space in your kitchen. So you can save a so much of room for other things in your kitchen. If not you can keep the equipment somewhere else (store room) when it is not being used. In future chapters you can get to know the way you have to store the product.

CHAPTER 3

HOW TO PROPERLY USE YOUR NINJA FOODI MULTICOOKER?

3.1 HOW EACH LID IS USED?

There are two main lids you can have with this Ninja Foodi Multi Cooker. One is the fixed air fryer lid. The other one is the detachable pressure cooking lid. There are some important facts you should know when operating these two lids. In this section you can get to know those things.

1. Air Frying Lid & Air Frying (Air Crisp also the same thing)

This lid is always stays with the equipment. So when you have something to air fry, follow these tips. First place the cooking pot inside the multi cooker. This is something you should know. Weather you pressure cook or air fry you have to use the cooking pot. After that place some parchment paper inside the basket. Then place the food item you want to air fry in the basket. After that put the basket in to the cooking pot. Now you are ready to go. Make sure you apply some oil on the food and turn on the cooker. Then select the air frying function. After that you can set the temperature and the cooking time. When the frying is done you can carefully take the food item out from the multi cooker and serve. "Important: During air frying make sure the air outlet has not been covered from a wall or another equipment". Also don't forget to close the air fryer lid when using "Air Crisp" mode.

2. Pressure Cooking Lid & Pressure Cooking

Here the situation is totally different from a traditional pressure cooker. The change is based on technology and safety. As mentioned earlier this machine does not release any pressure to outside during cooking. So when cooking you must put some water or liquid in to the cooking pot. Then you can place the food item you want to pressure cook in the basket. Then take the pressure cooking lid and close carefully. Make sure it seals the edges. Also make sure the pressure valve is sealed as well. After that turn on the cooker and select pressure function from the main controls. After that select the pressure level you want and set the "time" as well. Then you can start the cooking process. Once the pressure cooking is completed release all the built in pressure through the pressure valve and then open the lid. "Make sure all the pressure has been released before opening the lid".

There is a great safety functionality comes with the Ninja Foodi when it comes to pressure cooking. This comes with both ninja foodi multi cookers. Next to the pressure releasing valve you can see a "red button". **"If it stays out it means there is pressure inside the cooker. If it has gone down that means it has been depressurized. So it is safe to open".**

3.2 ALL IN ONE POT COOKING

This is one of the most important function you can try with the Ninja Foodi multi cooker. It is not that complicated to try. In simple words it is about cooking multiple things at once. For this you have to use the pressure cooking functionality. Let me explain this via an example. Let's say you want to cook vegetable rice and fried chicken together.

This is what you have to do,

a) Add some water or chicken broth to the cooking pot.
b) Then add the rice and chopped vegetable pieces.
c) Take the rack and place inside the cooking pot.
d) After that you can place the chicken slices on the rack.
e) Then turn on the multi cooker and select pressure function.
f) Select the pressure "Hi" and set the time to "5 minutes" and start pressure cooking.
g) After depressurizing open the lid and you can add some other vegetable such as coli flower or broccoli and you can place them on the rack as well.
h) You can apply some olive oil or soy sauce on the top of the chicken and vegetables.
i) Remove the pressure cooking lid.
j) Close the air frying lid.
k) Then select the "Broil" function and set the time for "10 minutes".
l) Once it is done you can enjoy the meal.

That was just a one example I have given to explain the functionality of the one pot cooking. So you are free to try your own recipes in this multi cooker.

3.3 QUICK PRESSURE RELEASE VS NATURAL PRESSURE RELEASE

In previous sections you might have gone through this topic. Let's dive deeper in to that topic. So as mentioned pressure cookers gain pressure inside them when cooking. Same principle applies to the Ninja Foodi multi cooker as well. So there are two ways you can control release the pressure.

1. Natural release

In this you don't have to interfere with the process. Just after pressure cooking you have to leave the appliance for 10 minutes. Then it will be depressurized. To verify that just observe the "red button" next to the pressure valve. If it has come up it means the inside pressure is high. So you should not open the lid. For natural pressure release just leave the appliance alone for 10 minutes after cooking. Then the "red button" will go down and then you can open the lid (please check the display as well as the red button before opening the lid). So that is all about natural pressure release.

2. Quick release

If you are in a rush and you don't have enough time to do the natural pressure release. So then you can go for the quick release. In this case also you have to wait until the pressure cooking is done. Then you can release the pressure valve manually from your fingers or using a stick. Using a stick is safer than using your finger. So let the whole pressure get out from the cooker. Then check out the red button again to make sure there are no any pressure inside it. Then you can open the lid.

3.4 CAN YOU COOK REGULAR MEALS IN THE NINJA FOODI?

Actually it is not a hard thing as you might have thought. You should consider two important things when it comes trying regular meals in your ninja foodi. That is the size of the meal and the way you want prepare it. Most of the time the space in the both ninja foodi models will be enough for majority of dishes. So it won't be a huge issue. As a plus point you can try the rack which comes with the equipment and try multiple food items at once. So in conclusion we can say that the ninja foodi will help you to recreate your ordinary dishes even more creatively and efficiently.

CHAPTER 4

HOW TO CLEAN & MAINTAIN YOUR NINJA FOODI MULTI COOKER

4.1 THE PROPER WAY TO CLEAN YOUR NINJA FOODI

Cleaning is really important for any appliance. Because it can decide the durability and the safety of it. Therefore proper cleaning is a must for any kitchen appliance. Let's get to know why and how you have to clean the Ninja Foodi Multi Cooker. It is not that hard to clean this item. Make a habit of cleaning this product after each use. You must unplug the appliance from power when cleaning. Also you mustn't put water in to electronic components. That could damage or even cause accidents. So be careful and mindful about that.

- ✓ For your comfort I will divide the cleaning process into few steps.
    1. First take out the cooking pot and the basket out with the rack.
    2. Then take a wash cloth with mildly warm water.
    3. Then soak it in the water and remove excess water.
    4. After that gently rub on the inside of the air fryer lid.
    5. Make sure you take out all the oil stains and remaining food particles from the heating element and fan.
    6. If it is difficult for you to reach any place use a small stick like chop stick and wrap the cloth around it.
    7. Then you can clean the heating element and its surrounded area.
    8. Make sure you won't damage any parts. Also don't pour water directly to the heating element.
    9. Then wipe the lid with a clean dry cloth and set aside.
    10. Now you can wash the cooking pot, basket and the rack with soap and water as usual.
    11. Let them dry.
    12. Now take the pressure cooking lid and turn upside down.
    13. You will notice an anti-clog cap just inside of the pressure valve.
    14. Just squeeze it and pull it lightly. It will come out.

15. Now you can wash inside of the lid and the anti-clog cap with soap & water.
16. Meanwhile you will find a silicon ring which has been placed inside the pressure lid for sealing purposes.
17. Take it out as well. Then wash it with soap and water.
18. After that take a wash cloth with mildly warm water.
19. Soak the cloth in the water and remove excess water. Then wipe the exterior and the edges of the Ninja Foodi.
20. Now turn the equipment backwards and take the condensation collector out. In there all the excess oils and the remaining liquids will be stored.
21. So take it out and clean with soap & water and let it dry.
22. Also pay your special attention to the air frying air out let as well.
23. Now you have cleaned everything perfectly well.
24. Let them dry and fix them all again. You are good to go.

So those are the main tips you need to consider when it comes to cleaning and maintaining the ninja foodi multi cooker.

4.2 HOW TO STORE YOUR NINJA FOODI?

This is really important as well as cleaning your ninja foodi. Because it can decide the durability as well as the efficiency of your cooker. Always let the equipment cool before moving it to a storage area. Keep in your mind that you can't close the ninja foodi with both lids at ones. So I would suggest to close the air frying lid (fixed lid) and keep the other lid (pressure cooking lid) next to the equipment facing downwards.

So if you are using the ninja foodi occasionally, then I would suggest to cover it from a large cloth or a plastic bag in order to save it from dust and other particles. If you are using the item more often you can place it in your kitchen where it doesn't get any water splashes or extreme heat. These simple tips can increase the durability of your product.

CHAPTER 5

TECHNOLOGY RELATED WITH NINJA FOODI MULTI COOKER

5.1 HOW TECHNOLOGY HAS BEEN USED IN NINJA FOODI?

As you can see Ninja Foodi Multi Cooker is not a traditional cooking appliance. It is a multipurpose cooker. So it's a blend of multiple technologies as well. Ninja Foodi Original comes with a 1400W unit. Ninja Foodi Deluxe comes with the 1760W unit. Both of these models use rapid energy conversion methods. Which means these machines are capable of transferring power equally towards different tasks. At the same time it will help you to save power as well. Because Ninja Foodi designers have considered on energy saving as well. That will be a huge plus point for you. Due to its multi cooking abilities as well as power saving capabilities.

5.2 WHAT IS TENDER CRISP TECHNOLOGY AND HOW TO USE IT?

You might have seen this in various articles and even in the product manual. So what is this? In simple words it is the combination of two technologies. By now you know that Ninja Foodi is capable of air frying as well as pressure cooking. From the phrase "tender crisp" you can get a clue regarding this technology. So it is like this. When you boil or pressure cook something it becomes tender. When you fry or air fry something it becomes crispy. This is how tendercrisp technology works. In here let's take fish filets for an example.

First you have to fill some water in to cooking pot. Then you can place the fish slices on the stainless steel rack and close the pressure cooking lid. Then you can start pressure cooking. When the cooking is done you don't have to move the fish anywhere. Now the fish slices have become **tender**. Then just apply some oil or some soy sauce on the fish slices and then close the multi cooker with the air frying lid.

Then you can select air crisp / air fry mode and cook them according to the recommended time in the recipe. When it is completed your fish is **crispier**. So now you have got the defined meaning of the **tender crispiness.** As a result of that your cooked fish slices will have the soft / tender texture in the middle as well as the crispy texture in the outside. So you can experience a next level taste variation in your **tender crisped** meals. That is what I can say about tender crisp technology in simple understandable language.

5.3 HOW TO PERFECTLY TENDERCRISP?

1. To properly tender crisp some dish you have to pay attention to some details. Let's go through those factors. The amount of water you put for pressure cooking plays a massive part in this process. Because it determines the quality of pressure cooking. So make sure you put the required amount of water to the time which has been mentioned in your recipe.
2. The next important fact is the shape of the food. If you are preparing poultry, meat or seafood make sure they are sliced or have maximized the surface area. We do that to absorb the maximum amount of heat.
3. Most of the time users will miss this part. That is the transition time. Air frying just after the pressure cooking might consume more electricity as well as the internal parts in the equipment. Therefore give it 5 – 10 minutes prior to air fry your food item. (Especially when using tender crisp function)

4. During the pressure cooking your do not need to apply any coating or oily layer. But when it comes to air frying you will have to apply some oil coating to gain the maximum crispiness in your food. So don't forget to do that part.
5. So by following above guidelines you could have a great dish which has been cooked with the tender crisp technology.

5.4 GENERAL TIPS ABOUT THE NINJA FOODI

1. Apart from that take all the standard precautions you should take while using an electronic appliance. Such like not handling the equipment with wet hands.
2. Keep away from heat and fire.
3. Follow the limits mentioned in the cooking pot.
4. Do not overuse the appliance. Give it breaks during a heavy use.
5. Close the air fryer lid while storing.
6. Do not try multiple functions at once.
7. Even though this is a multi-cooker still it can do one function at a given time (such as air crisp or pressure cook).
8. Do not try pressure cooking function with the air fryer lid on.
9. Also do not try the air fryer functions with the pressure cooker lid on.
10. Do not remove any screws or nuts. It'll void the warranty as well as may damage the equipment.

11. If there is some problem take it to an authorized dealer.
12. Treat it well, it will treat you the same.

CHAPTER 6

COMMON MISTAKES AND HOW TO AVOID THEM

1. Do not over crowd the basket.
2. Not thinking of cleaning properly each and every corner of the equipment.
3. Forget to rotate the portions while cooking.
4. Do not forget to check the water volume before pressure cooking.
5. Forgetting to put some oil to the food portion before air frying.
6. Not sealing the pressure releasing valve before starting pressure cooking.
7. Don't forget to put the silicon sealing ring prior to pressure cooking.
8. You should not over fill the cooking pot.
9. Don't all the variety of foods at the same time.
10. Not using the ninja foodi more often.
11. During washing do not use any rough brushes to remove the food remainings. That could damage the nonstick ceramic coating of the cooking pot.

CHAPTER 7 – BREAKFAST RECIPES

1. APPLE DUMPLINGS

Preparation Time: 10 Minutes

Cooking Time: 8 Minutes

Servings: 4

Ingredients:

- Chopped apples – 1 can
- Low sugar frosting – ¼ cup
- Crescent rolls – 1 pack (8 inch)

Instructions:

1. Place a crescent roll on the cutting board.
2. Place some apple mixture over the middle.

3. Then fold the roll.
4. Do the same thing to all the rolls.
5. Put a parchment paper over the air fryer basket.
6. Select air crisp function and set the temperature at 350F/ 177C.
7. Air fry for 5 minutes.
8. Then switch the sides over and air fry for another 3 minutes.
9. Take them out and let them cool for few minutes.
10. Put the frosting and serve.

Nutritional information per serving: Calories: 405, Fat: 15g, Sodium: 540mg, Fiber: 1g, Sugar: 25g, Carbohydrate 73g, Protein 2g.

2. AIR FRIED FISH MUFFINS

Preparation Time: 10 Minutes

Cooking Time: 20 Minutes

Servings: 2

Ingredients:

- Olive oil spray
- Chopped cod fish - 10oz / 283g
- Breadcrumbs – 2/3 cup
- Chopped cilantro – 3 tbsp
- Chili sauce – 2 tbsp
- Mayonnaise – 2 tbsp
- 1 Egg
- Salt – 1/8 tsp
- Powdered pepper – ¼ tsp

- 2 Lemons slices

Instructions:

1. Apply the olive oil spray to the air fryer basket of the ninja foodi.
2. Take bowl and mix breadcrumbs, fish, cilantro, chili sauce, cheese, pepper, egg and salt.
3. Then place the mixture in cupcake cases which is about 2.5 – 3.0 inch in size.
4. Apply olive oil on the fish cakes as well.
5. Select the air crisp option.
6. Set the temperature to 400F / 204C.
7. Cook for 10 minutes until the cakes get a brown color.
8. Serve with lemon slices.

Nutritional information per serving: Calories: 398, Fat: 15g, Sodium: 536mg, Fiber: 2.7g, Sugar: 9.5g, Carbohydrate 28g, Protein 35g.

3. AIR FRIED CHEESE BREAD

Preparation Time: 10 Minutes

Cooking Time: 8 Minutes

Servings: 1

Ingredients:

- Prepared pizza dough – 1 pack
- Butter – ½ cup
- Mozzarella cheese – 2 cups
- Any topping you like
- Crushed garlic – 1 teaspoon
- Dried fresh parsley – 1 pinch

Instructions:

1. Well mix the dough for 15 minutes.
2. Then keep it aside.
3. Take a bowl and add garlic, butter and parsley.
4. Mix well and apply on the dough.
5. Take the air frying basket and place the rack in it.
6. Place the dough on the rack.
7. Choose the air crisp option and set the temperature at 380F / 193C.
8. Then close the air frying lid.
9. Air fry for 5 minutes.
10. Open the lid and apply the second layer of butter mix.

11. Sprinkle some cheese over the dough and close the lid again.
12. Air fry for another 10 minutes until the cheese melts.
13. When adding your topping, you have to be careful not to overcook it.
14. Else you can enjoy the meal with cheese.

Nutritional information per serving: Calories: 182, Fat: 17g, Sodium: 231mg, Fiber: 1g, Carbohydrate 2g, Protein 6g.

4. AIR FRIED GARLIC BREAD

Preparation Time: 10 Minutes

Cooking Time: 20 Minutes

Servings: 4

Ingredients:

- Whole wheat flour – 1 cup / 128g / 4.5oz
- Shredded feta cheese – ¾ cup
- Powdered garlic – ¼ teaspoon
- Low fat yogurt - 2/3 cup (150g / 5.3oz)
- Olive oil – ½ tablespoon
- Baking powder – ½ teaspoon
- Salt – ¼ teaspoon

Instructions:

1. Take a bowl and add the dry ingredients.
2. Then put the yogurt to it and mix well.
3. Use your hands and form a smooth dough from the mixture.
4. Make sure the dough is roughly about 7.5 inch in width.
5. Grease the air fryer basket with olive oil.
6. Apply olive oil over the top of the dough as well.
7. Choose air crisp mode and set the temperature at 400F / 204C and cook for 12 minutes.
8. After that switch the dough sides and apply olive oil on the other side as well.
9. Put the cheese topping over the top.
10. Air fry for another 5 minutes.
11. Take it out let it cool and serve.

Nutritional information per serving: Calories: 220, Fat: 7g, Carbohydrate 25g, Protein 13g.

5. APPLE MIXED FLAT BREAD

Preparation Time: 10 Minutes

Cooking Time: 15 Minutes

Servings: 1

Ingredients:

- Whole wheat flour – ½ cup
- Brown sugar – 2 tablespoon
- Low fat yogurt - 3 tablespoon

For glaze

- Sugar powder - 1 tablespoon
- Water – ½ tablespoon
- Baking powder – 1 teaspoon
- Salt - ¼ teaspoon

- Cinnamon powder – ½ teaspoon
- ½ of a diced apple
- Butter – 1 tablespoon

Instructions:

1. Tale bowl and mix salt, brown sugar, cinnamon powder, baking powder and flour.
2. Include the butter as well and mix.
3. Then include the apples and further mix it.
4. Put the yogurt and mix with a fork.
5. Now you can use your hands to make a fine dough.
6. It shouldn't be thick.
7. Grease the air fryer basket with cooking spray and select air crisp mode then set the temperature at 375F / 190C.
8. Air fry for 12 minutes.
9. Till then mix the sugar powder with the water and make the glaze.
10. When the fritter is done and cooled place the glaze over it and serve.

Nutritional information per serving: Calories: 365, Fat: 12g, Carbohydrate 51g, Protein 10g.

6. AIR FRIED FISH ROLLS

Preparation Time: 15 Minutes

Cooking Time: 12 Minutes

Servings: 8

Ingredients:

- 8 Roll wrappers
- Shredded cabbage - 2 cups
- Olive oil – 2 tablespoon. Onions – ¼ cup
- Noodles – 1 small pack (3.5oz / 100g)
- Cooking spray
- Shredded carrots – ½ cup
- Shredded tuna fish – 85g / 3oz
- Soy sauce – 2 tablespoon
- Ginger paste – 1 teaspoon

Instructions:

1. Put the noodles in to the cooking pot and add some water.
2. Then select the sauté function and boil the noodles.
3. Once it is done take it out remove the excess water.
4. Then take a bowl and add carrots, cabbage, onions, shredded fish and soy sauce then mix well.
5. Put the mixture in to the wrapper and roll it up.
6. Apply cooking spray over the wrappers and place them on the air fryer basket.

7. Select air crisp mode then set the temperature at 375F / 190C and air fry for 8 minutes.
8. Switch sides ones after the first 4 minutes.

Nutritional information per serving: Calories: 134, Fat: 4g, Sodium: 362mg, Fiber: 1g, Sugar: 1g, Carbohydrate 22g, Protein 23g.

7. BATTER FRIED FISH

Preparation Time: 10 Minutes

Cooking Time: 12 Minutes

Servings: 4

Ingredients:

- All wheat flour – 1 cup
- Cornstarch – 2 tbsp
- Salt – 1 tsp
- Black pepper – ¼ tsp
- Cayenne pepper – 1 pinch
- Cod fish slices – 1 ½ lb / 680g
- Vegetable oil
- Baking soda – ½ tsp

- 1 Beaten egg
- Flour – ¾ cup
- Paprika – ½ tsp

Instructions:

1. Take mixing bowl and put flour 1 cup, baking soda and corn starch to a large bowl.
2. Include egg and mix till it gets smooth.
3. Cover the bowl and freeze it for 25 minutes.
4. Then add the remaining flour, salt, paprika, black and cayenne pepper then mix well.
5. Dip each fish slice in the batter and remove dripping batter and put it in to the seasoned flour.
6. Do this process to all the slices.
7. Select air crisp and set the temperature to 390F / 198C.
8. Apply vegetable oil over the fish slices as on the basket.
9. Air fry the fish slices for 10 minutes.
10. Serve with some lemon slices.

Nutritional information per serving: Calories: 389, Fat: 3g, Sodium: 823mg, Fiber: 2g, Sugar: 1g, Carbohydrate 47g, Protein 38g.

8. CRUNCHY BACON SLICES

Preparation Time: 10 Minutes

Cooking Time: 10 Minutes

Servings: 2

Ingredients:

- 10 Bacon slices

Instructions:

1. Place bacon in the ninja foodi basket.
2. Select air crisp mode and set temperature at 350F / 177C.
3. Air fry the bacon for 10 minutes.
4. Swap the excess oils from the bacon and serve.

Nutritional information per serving: Calories: 269, Fat: 20g, Sodium: 968mg, Carbohydrate 1g, Protein 19g.

9. CORN ZUCCHINI ROTI

Preparation Time: 15 Minutes
Cooking Time: 15 Minutes
Servings: 10
Ingredients:

- Zucchini – 1lb / 454g
- Corn kernels – 1 cup
- Grated cheese – ¼ cup
- Paprika – ¼ tsp

- 2 Eggs
- All-purpose flour – 1 cup
- Baking powder – 1 tsp
- Olive oil spray
- Sour cream
- Shredded onion – ¼ cup
- Minced garlic - 1 clove
- Parsley – 1 tbsp
- Salt – 1 tsp
- Black pepper – ½ tsp
- Dried basil – ½ tsp
- Oregano – ½ tsp

Instructions:

1. Choose air crisp mode and preheat the ninja foodi to 370F / 188C.
2. Slice the zucchini.
3. Move the zucchini slices to the clean towel and squeeze the water out of them.
4. Put zucchini in to a bowl and put cheese, corn, onion, garlic, parsley, pepper, salt, oregano, eggs and paprika.
5. Then mix them well.
6. After that put flour and baking powder as well.
7. Create 10 flat patties from the mixture.
8. Apply cooking spray to the basket and to the patties.

9. Flip sides of the patties during the half way and apply oil on that side as well.
10. Then air fry for another 5 minutes.
11. Take them out and serve.

Nutritional information per serving: Calories: 95, Fat: 6g, Sodium: 319mg, Fiber: 2g, Sugar: 2g, Carbohydrate 7g, Protein 5g.

10. CHICKEN PATTIES

Preparation Time: 10 Minutes

Cooking Time: 30 Minutes

Servings: 6

Ingredients:

- 12 Corn tortillas
- Shredded Cheese – 1 ½ cups
- Steamed Diced Chicken – 1 ½ cups
- Tomato Sauce – 2 cups

Instructions:

1. Select air crisp mode and preheat the ninja foodi at 400F / 204C.

2. Grease the basket with cooking spray and apply some on the tortillas as well.
3. Air fry each side for 3 minutes.
4. Put the chicken over the top of the tortillas.
5. Then add the sauce as well.
6. After that put the shredded cheese and then roll the tortilla.
7. Put them in to the basket and air fry for 20 minutes at 325F / 163C.
8. Then open the lid and put some cheese on the top and select broil option and cook for another 3 minutes until the cheese melts.
9. Take them out.
10. Let them cool and serve.

Nutritional information per serving: Calories: 357, Fat: 14g, Sodium: 59mg, Fiber: 5g, Sugar: 2g, Carbohydrate 28g, Protein 28g.

11. CHEESY HAM SANDWICH WITH HOT SAUCE

Preparation Time: 2 Minutes

Cooking Time: 8 Minutes

Servings: 1

Ingredients:

- Ham - 4 slices
- BBQ sauce – 1 tablespoon
- Feta cheese – 3oz
- Butter– 2 teaspoons
- Brown bread – 2 slices

Instructions:

1. Apply butter on each side of the bread slices.

2. Take one bread slice and put a ham slice, bbq sauce, cheese, another ham slice and the other bread slice.
3. Choose air crisp mode.
4. Put the sandwich in the basket and set the temperature to 375F / 190C.
5. Cook for 10 minutes.
6. Turn slides after 5 minutes.
7. Continue air frying for another 3 minutes.
8. Let it cool and serve.

Nutritional information per serving: Calories: 622, Fat: 43g, Sodium: 1581mg, Fiber: 3g, Sugar: 1g, Carbohydrate 25g, Protein 34g.

12. CLASSIC BREAKFAST

Preparation Time: 10 Minutes

Cooking Time: 11 Minutes

Servings: 6

Ingredients:

- Diced onion – ¾ cup
- Olive oil – 1 tablespoon
- Salt - ½ teaspoon
- Shredded cheese – ¾ cup
- 3 Bread slices
- Sausage – ½ lb / 227g
- 5 Sliced mushrooms
- 8 Scrambled eggs

- Vegetable cream soup – ¼ cup

Instructions:

1. Switch on the ninja foodi and select sauté function.
2. Put onions, olive oil and sausage to the cooking pot and cook.
3. During the half way put sliced mushrooms continue cooking.
4. When the sausage is brown stop the cooking.
5. Take a bowl and mix an egg and add to the cooking pot.
6. Add some salt, cheese, vegetable soup cream.
7. Mix them well.
8. Close the air frying lid and choose air crisp function.
9. Select air crisp mode and cook for 5 minutes at 390F / 198C.
10. Sprinkle some remaining cheese and serve with bread.

Nutritional information per serving: Calories: 294, Fat: 22g, Sodium: 681mg, Sugar: 1g, Carbohydrate 3g, Protein 17g.

13. DELICIOUS FILLED PEPPERS

Preparation Time: 5 Minutes

Cooking Time: 13 Minutes

Servings: 2

Ingredients:

- 1 Bell pepper (cut in to half)
- Olive oil – 1 tea spoon
- Salt and pepper – 1 pinch
- 4 Eggs

Instructions:

1. First cut the bell peppers in half and remove seeds.
2. Then it should appear like cups.
3. Put two eggs in to one half.

4. Put the salt and pepper as needed.
5. Place them in the ninja foodi.
6. You can either place them on the basket or on the rack.
7. Choose air crisp mode.
8. Close the lid and cook for 12 minutes at 390F / 198C.
9. When it is done take it out let cool and enjoy the meal.

Nutritional information per serving: Calories: 164, Fat: 10g, Sodium: 146mg, Fiber: 1g, Sugar: 2g, Carbohydrate 4g, Protein 12g.

14. ENERGETIC CHICKEN NOODLE THICK SOUP

Preparation Time: 10 Minutes

Cooking Time: 30 Minutes

Servings: 4

Ingredients:

- Chicken drumsticks – 1 ½ lb / 680g
- 1 Diced onion
- Chopped celery - 1 stalk
- Chicken stock - 6 cups
- Olive oil – 1 tbsp
- Egg noodles – 8oz
- Salt
- Powdered black pepper

- Minced garlic - 4 cloves
- 6 Chopped button mushrooms
- 1 carrots

Instructions:

1. Select the saute function in ninja foodi.
2. Then put the garlic, mushroom, carrots, celery, salt, pepper and onion.
3. Stop the saute function.
4. Once it is done include the chicken stock.
5. Put chicken to the pot and pressure cook it under high pressure for 8 minutes.
6. Shred the chicken and mix with the soup.
7. Use the saute function again and boil the soup.
8. Add the noodles and further cook it.
9. Put salt & pepper and lime juice as desired.
10. Enjoy the delicious soup.

Nutritional information per serving: Calories: 535, Fat: 13g, Sodium: 346mg, Fiber: 4g, Sugar: 6g, Carbohydrate 53g, Protein 52g.

15. FRIED BROWN BREAD STICKS

Preparation Time: 20 Minutes

Cooking Time: 1 Hour

Servings: 12

Ingredients:
- 4 Mixed eggs
- Milk – ½ cup
- Whipping cream – 1 cup
- Cinnamon – 3 tablespoon
- Toasted bread (cut in to strips) – 12 slices
- Powdered sugar – 2 tablespoon (for topping)
- Maple syrup - 4 tablespoon
- Melted butter – 4 tablespoon

- Vanilla extract – 1 teaspoon
- Powdered sugar – ½ cup

Instructions:

1. Take bowl and put milk, eggs, whip cream and butter.
2. Mix them well.
3. Take another bowl and put sugar and cinnamon and well mix them.
4. Take one bread slice and dip in the egg mixture.
5. Then dip in the sugar mixture.
6. Straightly move it to the ninja foodi basket.
7. Make sure to have a single layer.
8. Select air crisp function.
9. Cook at 370F / 188C for 8 minutes.
10. Flip the bread slices from time to time.
11. Sprinkle some sugar and maple syrup over the top and serve.

Nutritional information per serving: Calories: 331, Fat: 20g, Sodium: 277mg, Fiber: 2g, Sugar: 15g, Carbohydrate 34g, Protein 6g.

16. FRIED SALMON

Preparation Time: 5 Minutes

Cooking Time: 7 Minutes

Servings: 2

Ingredients:

- 2 Salmon fillets
- Paprika – 2 tablespoons
- Salt & pepper
- Olive oil – 2 tablespoons
- Lime slices

Instructions:

1. Take your fish fillets and apply olive oil, paprika, salt & pepper and over them.
2. Move the fillets to air frying basket of ninja foodi.
3. Select air crisp mode.
4. Cook at 390F / 198C and cook for 7 minutes.
5. Take them out and serve with lime slices.

Nutritional information per serving: Calories: 288, Fat: 18.9g, Sodium: 81mg, Fiber: 0.8g, Sugar: 0.3g, Carbohydrate 1.5g, Protein 28g.

17. FRIED CHEESE TOAST

Preparation Time: 5 Minutes

Cooking Time: 5 Minutes

Servings: 2

Ingredients:

- Cheddar – 4oz / 113g
- Butter – 2 tbsp
- 4 Bread slices

Instructions:

1. Select air crisp mode
2. Preheat the ninja foodi to 350F / 177C.
3. Apply butter on each side of bread slice.
4. Then place cheese in the middle.

5. Cook for 5 minutes until the cheese melts.
6. Take it out and serve.

Nutritional information per serving: Calories: 481, Fat: 1g, Sodium: 743mg, Fiber: 2g, Sugar: 4g, Carbohydrate 29g, Protein 18g.

18. HOME FRIES

Preparation Time: 15 Minutes

Cooking Time: 20 Minutes

Servings: 6

Ingredients:

- 4 Shredded potatoes
- 1 Diced onion
- Pepper – ½ teaspoon
- Cheese shredded – 1 cup
- Salt – 1 teaspoon

Instructions:

1. Take the potato and put in to a water bowl for 25 minutes.
2. Then remove the water from potatoes. (use paper towels for that)
3. Move potatoes to a mixing bowl and add onions, pepper and salt.
4. After well mixing them, move the mixture in the cooking oil greased basket.
5. Choose air crisp mode and set the temperature to 400F / 204C and cook for 20 minutes.
6. Make sure you stir them every 5 minutes.
7. You can put a cheese topping and cook for additional 3 minutes till it melts.
8. Enjoy the dish.

Nutritional information per serving: Calories: 84, Fat: 6g, Sodium: 506mg, Fiber: 1g, Sugar: 1g, Carbohydrate 2g, Protein 5g.

19. HOMEMADE SWEET POTATO BITES

Preparation Time: 5 Minutes

Cooking Time: 25 Minutes

Servings: 3

Ingredients:

- 1 Sweet potato (cut in to slices) – 12oz / 340g
- Olive oil – 1 tablespoon
- Dried oregano – ½ teaspoon
- Red pepper powder – ½ teaspoon
- Black pepper – ¼ teaspoon
- Thyme – ¼ teaspoon
- Sugar – ½ tablespoon
- Smoked paprika – 1 teaspoon

- Salt – ½ teaspoon
- Garlic powder – ½ teaspoon
- Onion powder – ½ teaspoon

Instructions:

1. Move the sweet potato pieces in to a bowl and put olive oil as well.
2. Then mix them well.
3. Include the seasoning ingredients as well and keep mixing.
4. Select air crisp function.
5. Place them in the basket of ninja foodi and cook at 400F / 204C for 15 minutes.
6. Let it cool and then serve.

Nutritional information per serving: Calories: 220, Fat: 7g, Carbohydrate 38g, Protein 3g.

20. HOT DOGS WITH MELTED CHEESE

Preparation Time: 5 Minutes

Cooking Time: 10 Minutes

Servings: 4

Ingredients:

- 4 Hot dog buns
- Chili sauce
- 4 Sausages
- Cheese – ¼ cup

Instructions:

1. Apply some cooking spray in the basket of your ninja foodi and place the sausages in it.
2. Select air crisp mode.

3. Set the temperature to 375F / 190C and cook for 5 minutes. Switch sides as required.
4. Then take the sausages out and put the hot dog buns in to the basket.
5. Slice them half and heat them for 2 minutes at the same temperature.
6. Put one sausage to each bun and add cheese as well.
7. Cook the hot dog bun for 5 minutes till cheese melts and serve with sauce.

Nutritional information per serving: Calories: 280, Fat: 10g, Sodium: 569mg, Fiber: 1g, Sugar: 5g, Carbohydrate 34g, Protein 11g.

21. HEALTHY MORNING CASSEROLE

Preparation Time: 10 Minutes

Cooking Time: 15 Minutes

Servings: 8

Ingredients:

- Grilled sausage – 1lb / 454g
- Sliced onion – ¼ cup
- 1 Bell pepper (diced)
- 8 Eggs
- Shredded cheese – ½ cup
- Salt – ½ teaspoon

Instructions:
1. Switch on the ninja foodi and select the saute option.
2. Put the sausage to the cooking pot and let it cook till it gets brown.
3. Then include the pepper and onion to the mixture and stir well.
4. Then turn off the saute function.
5. Take your air frying pan and move the sausage mixture to it.
6. Don't forget to apply some oil on the pan prior to move the mixture.
7. Add cheese as the topping.
8. Then pour the beaten eggs over the mixture.
9. Take the rack and use its low position and keep the pan on it.
10. Set the time as 15 minutes and use air crisp option.
11. Set the temperature at 390F/198C.
12. Once it is completed serve the dish.

Nutritional information per serving: Calories: 283, Fat: 23g, Sodium: 681mg, Sugar: 2g, Carbohydrate 3g, Protein 15g.

22. HOT CHICKEN & VEGE BITES

Preparation Time: 10 Minutes

Cooking Time: 20 Minutes

Servings: 4

Ingredients:

- 4 Chicken thighs (skin & bones removed)
- Soy sauce - 2 tablespoon
- Powdered ginger – 1 teaspoon
- Olive oil – 1 tablespoon
- Coleslaw – 1 pack

Instructions:

1. Cut the chicken in to bite size pieces.
2. Select the saute function of your ninja foodi and put some olive oil to the cooking pot.

3. Move the chicken to the pot.
4. Cook in saute mode under hi heat for 8 minutes.
5. Then turn the heat in to medium and add the coleslaw, soy sauce, and ginger.
6. Stir this well.
7. Continue stir cooking for another 10 minutes and turn off the saute and move to a dish and serve.

Nutritional information per serving: Calories: 198, Fat: 12g, Sodium: 322mg, Fiber: 1g, Sugar: 4g, Carbohydrate 5g, Protein 18g.

23. KETOGENIC EGG MUFFIN

Preparation Time: 5 Minutes
Cooking Time: 9 Minutes
Servings: 1

Muffin pan is required (silicon or steel).

Ingredients:

- Water – ½ tbsp
- Salt & pepper – 1tsp
- 4 Egg whites
- Shredded cheese – 4 tbsp

Instructions:

1. Take a mixing bowl and add egg whites, water salt & pepper.

2. Mix them well.
3. Take the muffin tray and apply some oil on it.
4. Pour the mixture in to muffin tins and place them in the muffin tray.
5. Put the shredded cheese over the muffin cups.
6. Place the muffin tray in the ninja foodi.
7. Select the air crisp function in the ninja foodi and set the temperature to 370F / 188C and cook for 15 minutes.
8. Let it cool and serve.

Nutritional information per serving: Calories: 207, Fat: 12g, Sodium: 592mg, Sugar: 8g, Carbohydrate 15g, Protein 9g.

24. LOW STARCH FRIED EGG BITES

Preparation Time: 10 Minutes

Cooking Time: 10 Minutes

Servings: 4

Ingredients:

- 4 Eggs
- Milk – 4 teaspoon
- Shredded cheese – ¼ cup
- Salt and pepper
- ½ Diced onion
- ½ Diced bell pepper
- 4 Cooked bacon strips

Instructions:

1. For this also you have to use the air frying function of your ninja foodi.
2. Take 4 muffin cases and place them in the basket.
3. Then put one egg to each case.
4. Pour 1 tsp of milk to each tin as well.
5. Add some onions and pepper over the top as well.
6. Put salt & pepper also.
7. Select air crisp mode.
8. Set the temperature as 300F / 148C and cook for 12 minutes.
9. Cool them and serve.

Nutritional information per serving: Calories: 184, Fat: 15g, Sodium: 255mg, Fiber: 1g, Sugar: 1g, Carbohydrate 3g, Protein 10g.

25. MAYO BURGER

Preparation Time: 10 Minutes

Cooking Time: 6 Minutes

Servings: 6

Ingredients:

- Diced cheese – 8oz / 227g
- Sesame seeds – 2 tsp
- Chopped beef – 1lb / 454g
- Sliced Dill pickles

- Shredded lettuce
- 1 Chopped onion
- 6 Tortillas
- Mayonnaise

Instructions:
1. Select the saute function of your ninja foodi.
2. Put beef and onion to the cooking pot.
3. Cook it beef turns in to light brown color.
4. Remove the grease of the meat.
5. Take a tortilla and put the beef, pickle, cheese and mayo on it.
6. Do the same process for three layers.
7. You can take the air fryer pan to cook the burger from here onwards.
8. Put one water cup to the cooking pot of the ninja foodi.
9. Close with the pressure cooking lid.
10. Then pressure cook the burger at high pressure for 5 minutes and do the quick pressure release.
11. Remove the pressure cooking lid. And drain the water in the cooking pot carefully.
12. Place the cooking pot and basket with the burger.
13. Close the air frying lid and select air crisp mode and set the temperature to 400F / 204C and cook for 3 minutes.
14. Serve with some lettuce.

Nutritional information per serving: Calories: 548, Fat: 23g, Sodium: 1008mg, Fiber: 3g, Carbohydrate 20g, Protein 27g.

26. NUTRITIOUS MORNING PUFF

Preparation Time: 10 Minutes

Cooking Time: 15 Minutes

Servings: 8

Ingredients:

- Ground sausage – 1lb / 454g
- Shredded onion – ¼ cup
- 8 Eggs
- Shredded cheese - ½ cup
- Salt – ½ tsp
- 1 Diced bell pepper

Instructions:

1. Select the saute option in your ninja foodi.
2. Add sausages, onion and pepper then cook until veggies are cooked and sausage is fried.
3. Stop the saute function.
4. Take the air fryer 8 inch pan and put the sausage mixture to it. Grease it with cooking spray before adding mixture.
5. Then add a cheese topping.
6. Now pour the mixed eggs over the cheese.
7. Sprinkle some salt over it.
8. Take the rack and place it in the low position in the ninja foodi and keep the pan on the top.
9. Select air crisp mode.

10. Set the temperature at 390F / 198C.
11. And cook for 15 minutes.
12. Serve it when it reduces the heat.
13. Enjoy the dish.

Nutritional information per serving: Calories: 282, Fat: 23g, Sodium: 682mg, Sugar: 2g, Carbohydrate 2g, Protein 15g.

27. NINJA FRIED POTATOES

Preparation Time: 10 Minutes

Cooking Time: 20 Minutes

Servings: 6

Ingredients:

- 4 Potatoes
- Rosemary – 1 tablespoon
- Olive oil – ½ tablespoon

Instructions:

1. First cut potatoes in half.
2. The slice them in to bite size pieces.
3. Take a bowl and put potatoes, rosemary and olive oil.
4. Well mix them.

5. Choose air crisp function.
6. Place in the basket and set the temperature at 350F / 177C.
7. Cook for 20 minutes and enjoy.

Nutritional information per serving: Calories: 198, Fat: 7g, Sodium: 414mg, Sugar: 1g, Carbohydrate 30g, Protein 3g.

28. PRESSURE COOKED RICE

Preparation Time: 5 Minutes

Cooking Time: 2 Minutes

Servings: 4

Ingredients:

- Rice – 2 cups
- Salt as required
- Water – 2 ½ cups

Instructions:

1. Put the rice cups in to the cooking pot.
2. Add water cups.
3. Then put the pressure cooking lid and close the pressure valve.

4. Select pressure function and set up hi pressure for 2 minutes.
5. Go for quick release if you have less time. Or else go for the natural release (it will take 10 minutes).
6. Remove the lid.
7. Serve the rice.

Nutritional information per serving: Calories: 337, Fat: g, Sodium: 59mg, Fiber: 1g, Carbohydrate 73g, Protein 6g.

29. PORK TACOS

Preparation Time: 25 Minutes

Cooking Time: 1 Hour

Servings: 10

Ingredients:

- Pork – 3lb / 1.36kg
- Orange juice – 1 ½ cups
- Chili powder – 2 teaspoons
- Sliced onion
- 3 Jalapenos (sliced)
- Garlic – 6 cloves
- Sour cream
- Shredded cabbage

- Pickled onion
- Chili sauce
- Powdered black pepper - 2 teaspoons
- Cumin powder - 1 teaspoons
- 1 Cinnamon stick
- Dried oregano – 1 tablespoon
- Powdered cloves – ½ teaspoons
- Salt – 2 ½ teaspoons
- Tortillas

Instructions:

1. Take a bowl and put pork, chili powder, orange juice, garlic, jalapenos, onion and other mentioned seasonings and mix well.
2. Put the mixture in to the cooking pot and close with the pressure cooking lid.
3. Set it to high pressure and cook for 35 minutes.
4. You can go for a quick release for 10 minutes natural release. (You must check the red button and the display before opening the lid. Never open the lid when there is pressure inside.)
5. Once it is done remove the pepper and spices.
6. Put the pork in to a bowl.
7. Then shred the meat.
8. Put ¾ cup of the cooked liquid in the cooking pot to the pork bowl and mix well.
9. Place the mixture in to an air frying pan.

10. Then select saute the pork till it gets crispy for 10 – 25 minutes.
11. Once it is done move to a separate dish.
12. Select air crisp function and cook the tortillas for 5 minutes at 250F / 121C.
13. Then put the pork mixture, sour cream, cabbage, chili sauce and pickled onion to the tortilla and serve.

Nutritional information per serving: Calories: 140, Fat: 6g, Sodium: 410mg, Fiber: 8g, Carbohydrate 13g, Protein 18g.

30. STIR FRIED BEANS

Preparation Time: 5 Minutes

Cooking Time: 25 Minutes

Servings: 12

Ingredients:

- Crushed garlic - 2 Cloves
- Pepper – 1 teaspoon
- Seasoning – 2 tablespoon
- Water - 6 Cups
- Sliced beans – 1lb / 454g
- Sliced onion – ½ cup
- Salt – 1 teaspoon

Instructions:
1. Put the beans, onion, garlic and seasonings to the ninja foodi.
2. Put water cups to the pot as well.
3. Close the pressure cooking lid.
4. Set pressure to hi and cook for 25 minutes.
5. When the cooking is done. Go for a natural pressure release (leave for 10 minutes).
6. Check the red button and the display then open the lid and serve the dish.

Nutritional information per serving: Calories: 142, Fat: 1g, Sodium: 308mg, Fiber: 6g, Sugar: 1g, Carbohydrate 26g, Protein 8g.

31. STANDARD BREAKFAST

Preparation Time: 10 Minutes
Cooking Time: 11 Minutes
Servings: 6
Ingredients:
- Diced onion – ¾ cup
- Olive oil – 1 tablespoon
- 5 Sliced mushrooms
- Ground sausage – ½ lb / 227g
- 8 Scrambled eggs
- Vegetable soup cream – ¼ cup

- Salt – ½ teaspoon
- Shredded cheese – ¾ cup

Instructions:

1. Turn on and select the saute in your ninja foodi.
2. Then put olive oil, onions, and sausage to the cooking pot.
3. Put the mushrooms to the pot and cook for another few minutes and stop the saute function.
4. Pour the scrambled eggs to the meat.
5. Add cheese, salt and add vegetable cream to it.
6. Mix everything well.
7. Select air crisp mode.
8. Close the air frying lid and set the temperature to 390F / 198C and cook for 5 minutes.
9. Let it cool and serve.

Nutritional information per serving: Calories: 294, Fat: 22g, Sodium: 681mg, Sugar: 1g, Carbohydrate 3g, Protein 18g.

32. SMOOTH FRITTATA

Preparation Time: 10 Minutes

Cooking Time: 8 Minutes

Servings: 4

Ingredients:

- 3 Eggs
- Sliced bell pepper
- Shredded cheese – 2 tablespoon
- Thyme – ¼ teaspoon
- Salt – ¼ teaspoon
- Pepper – 1/8 teaspoon
- Cooking spray
- Diced onions – ¼ cup

- Milk – 2 tablespoon
- 3 Halved tomatoes
- Dried tomatoes – 1 tablespoon

Instructions:
1. Use the air crisp function in the ninja foodi.
2. Preheat the ninja foodi at 350F / 177C.
3. Take a bowl and put eggs and other ingredients.
4. Then mix them well.
5. Take the air fryer pan (4 inch or any size you have)
6. Put the egg mixture to it.
7. Place it in the basket and cook for 8 minutes.
8. Then let it cool slice and serve.

Nutritional information per serving: Calories: 93, Fat: 6g, Sodium: 246mg, Fiber: 1g, Sugar: 2g, Carbohydrate 3g, Protein 8g.

33. STIR FRIED SAUSAGES WITH MASHED POTATOES

Preparation Time: 10 Minutes

Cooking Time: 12 Minutes

Servings: 5

Ingredients:

- 2 Sliced fried sausage
- 5 Potatoes cut in to cubes
- Salt & pepper as required
- 1 Sliced onion
- Minced garlic – 1 tablespoon
- Olive oil – 2 tablespoon
- Garlic salt – ½ teaspoon

Instructions:

1. Take a bowl and put onions, potatoes, garlic, olive oil, seasonings and sausages.
2. Mix them well and move to the olive oil greased basket.
3. Select air crisp mode.
4. Set the temperature to 400F / 204C and cook for 12 minutes.
5. Cook all the mixture in batches. Don't over load the basket.
6. Then you can serve them.

Nutritional information per serving: Calories: 229, Fat: 10g, Sodium: 377mg, Fiber: 6g, Sugar: 1g, Carbohydrate 28g, Protein 8g.

34. STEAMED TENDER CHICKEN BUN

Preparation Time: 10 Minutes

Cooking Time: 20 Minutes

Servings: 8

Ingredients:

- Chicken breasts – 2lb / 907g
- 8 Buns
- Water – 4 cups
- Dressing & seasoning
- Chopped parsley - 1 tsp
- Chopped dill – 1 ½ tsp
- Lime juice – 1 tbsp
- Garlic powder – ¼ tsp

- Salt & pepper
- Butter – 4 tbsp
- Mayonnaise – 1/3 cup
- Mustard – 1 tbsp
- Diced celery – 2 ribs

Instructions:

1. Put the chicken in to the cooking pot and add water 4 cups as well.
2. Pressure cook for 8 minutes at "Hi" pressure. (Close from the pressure cooking lid. Make sure the pressure valve is sealed).
3. Take the chicken out and shred it using a fork and knife.
4. Now put the chicken in to a mixing bowl and add celery, mayo and mustard then mix them well.
5. Include garlic powder as well.
6. Then put parsley leaves, dill and lime juice and mix.
7. Add salt & pepper as desired.
8. Cut the buns in half.
9. Now apply butter on each slice of the bun.
10. Put the chicken mixture on it.
11. Choose air crisp function.
12. You can cook for another 5 minutes at 250F / 120C.
13. Now serve the dish.

Nutritional information per serving: Calories: 196, Fat: 10g, Sodium: 220mg, Carbohydrate 15g, Protein 24g.

35. STRACHY LOW CARB SOUP

Preparation Time: 10 Minutes

Cooking Time: 35 Minutes

Servings: 6

Ingredients:

- Chopped potatoes – 1 ½ lb / 680g
- 1 Diced onion
- Whip cream – 1 cup
- 2 Bay leaves
- 2 Chopped green onions
- Salt & ground black pepper to taste
- Chicken stock – 4 cups
- Minced garlic – 6 cloves

- Chopped bacon – 6 slices

Instructions:

1. Put the bacon in pot and select saute option and cook for 5 minutes.
2. Remove the excess fat from a paper towel.
3. Put onion to the cooking pot and use saute for 2 minutes.
4. Include garlic and bay leaves.
5. Then saute for another minute.
6. Once it is done you can add the chicken stock to the pot.
7. Now add the potatoes and close with the pressure cooking lid. (Make sure the pressure valve is sealed).
8. Pressure cook at "Hi" for 3 minutes. And give it a natural pressure release (10 – 15 minutes).
9. Remove the bay leaves and pour the potato mixture in to blender and add salt and pepper as well as whip cream.
10. Sprinkle the bacon and grated cheese over the soup and serve.

Nutritional information per serving: Calories: 320, Fat: 22g, Sodium: 240mg, Fiber: 3g, Sugar: 1g, Carbohydrate 21g, Protein 10g.

36. SWEET POTATO SQUASH

Preparation Time: 10 Minutes

Cooking Time: 20 Minutes

Servings: 3

Ingredients:

- Potatoes (peeled 7 sliced) – 3 lb / 1.36kg
- Water – 1 cup
- Sour cream – ¼ cup
- Butter – 4 tbsp
- Garlic salt– 1 tsp
- Milk - ½ cup

Instructions:

1. Put the potatoes in to the ninja foodi cooking pot.

2. Add water cup.
3. Put pressure cooker lid and seal the pressure valve.
4. Select the pressure level "Hi" and cook for 10 minutes.
5. Do the natural pressure release. (Wait for 10 minutes. Check the red pressure indicating button as well as the display before opening the lid).
6. Take the potatoes out and put them in a bowl and mash them using a spoon.
7. Include the other spices and mix well.
8. Put the mixture back in to the cooking pot and close the air frying lid.
9. Select air crisp mode and set the temperature at 350F / 177C.
10. Cook for 5 minutes and serve.

Nutritional information per serving: Calories: 231, Fat: 12g, Sodium: 154mg, Fiber: 3g, Sugar: 2g, Carbohydrate 28g, Protein 5g.

37. STEAMED OATS WITH BROWN SUGAR SYRUP

Preparation Time: 5 Minutes

Cooking Time: 35 Minutes

Servings: 6

Ingredients:

- Sliced oats – 2 cups
- Water – 3 ½ cups
- Vanilla extract – 1 teaspoon
- Sliced banana
- Berries
- Toasted sliced almonds
- Milk - 2cups
- Powdered cinnamon – ½ teaspoon

- Salt – ½ teaspoon
- Maple syrup – 2 tablespoon

Instructions:
1. Take a bowl and mix oats, water, cinnamon, milk and salt.
2. Put them in to the cooking pot of the ninja foodi.
3. Close with the pressure cooker lid.
4. Set pressure as "Hi" and cook for 5 minutes.
5. Choose the natural pressure release (this time leave it for 18 minutes).
6. After removing the lid add maple syrup, vanilla, banana, almonds and berries.
7. Then you can serve the dish.

Nutritional information per serving: Calories: 406, Fat: 6.2g, Sodium: 342mg, Fiber: 5.3g, Carbohydrate 78g, Protein 10g.

38. SPICY POTATOES WITH FRIED EGGS

Preparation Time: 15 Minutes

Cooking Time: 35 Minutes

Servings: 6

Ingredients:

- Olive oil – 1 tablespoon
- Butter – 1 tablespoon
- Sliced bacon – ½ lb / 227g
- 1 Sliced bell pepper (green)
- Minced garlic - 2 cloves
- Dried oregano – 1 teaspoon
- Cayenne – ¼ teaspoon
- Salt
- ½ a chopped onion
- 1 Sliced bell pepper (red)
- Powdered black pepper
- Slices potatoes – 1lb / 454g
- Vegetable broth – ½ cup
- Chopped parsley – 1 tablespoon
- 2 Eggs

Instructions:

1. Turn on the ninja foodi and select the saute mode.
2. Put oil and butter to the cooking pot.
3. Then add bacon, onion and peppers.
4. Cook till they become tender.

5. Include garlic, oregano and cayenne as well.
6. Let them cook for 2 minutes.
7. Stop the saute function
8. Now put the potatoes and vegetable broth to the pot.
9. Close with the pressure cooking lid.
10. Set the pressure to "high" and cook for 12 minutes.
11. Once the pressure cooking is done, do a quick pressure release
12. Remove the pressure cooking lid and change the mode back to saute.
13. Stir cook until the broth is evaporated.
14. Do this for 2 minutes.
15. Serve with steamed eggs. Also sprinkle some parsley over the dish and enjoy.

Nutritional information per serving: Calories: 385, Fat: 23g, Sodium: 756mg, Fiber: 18g, Sugar: 5g, Carbohydrate 45g, Protein 36g.

39. SIMPLE RISOTTO

Preparation Time: 10 Minutes

Cooking Time: 15 Minutes

Servings: 4

Ingredients:

- Chicken broth – 4 cups.
- Thyme leaves – 1 tablespoons
- Rice – 2 cups
- White wine – ¼ cup
- Shredded parmesan – ¾ cup
- Salt
- Butter – 2 tablespoons
- 1 Chopped onion

- Minced garlic – 3 cloves
- Powdered black pepper

Instructions:

1. First heat up the chicken broth.
2. Set the ninja foodi to saute mode and pour the broth to the cooking pot and cook for 5 minutes.
3. After that remove the broth another dish and keep aside.
4. Put the cooking pot back to the ninja foodi.
5. Add butter and onion then set the saute mode and cook for 5 minutes.
6. Then add the garlic and thyme. Then cook for another 5 minutes.
7. Now put the rice and stir for 2 minutes.
8. Add the wine and cook for another 2 minutes then turn off the saute function.
9. Now put the broth in to the rice and close with the pressure cooking lid.
10. Set the pressure high and cook for 8 minutes.
11. After that do a quick pressure release.
12. Remove the lid and add cheese, salt and pepper then serve.

Nutritional information per serving: Calories: 166, Fat: 7g, Sodium: 320mg, Fiber: 0.3g, Sugar: 0.1g, Carbohydrate 19g, Protein 5g.

40. STEAK SUBMARINE

Preparation Time: 10 Minutes

Cooking Time: 30 Minutes

Servings: 5

Ingredients:

- Olive oil – 1 tablespoon
- 1 Sliced bell pepper (green)
- Powdered black pepper
- Sliced steak – 1 lb / 454g
- Cheese - 6 slices
- 5 Hoagie rolls
- 1 Sliced bell pepper (orange)
- 1 Sliced onion

- Dried oregano – ½ teaspoon
- Salt

Instructions:

1. Select the saute mode and add oil.
2. Then add peppers, onion and oregano.
3. Add salt & pepper cook till onion gets softer for 5 minutes.
4. Put the beef to the cooking pot.
5. Turn off the saute mode and close the lid with the pressure cooking lid.
6. Set the pressure as "High" and cook for 8 minutes.
7. When it is done go for a natural pressure release.(leave it for 10 minutes after finishing the pressure cooking. You must check the "red button and display to make sure it has been depressurized).
8. Put the cheese over the steak mixture and mix well.
9. Close again from the lid and just let the cheese melt.
10. Put the mixture in to the hoagie rolls and serve.

Nutritional information per serving: Calories: 1070, Fat: 43g, Sodium: 3880mg, Fiber: 7g, Sugar: 12g, Carbohydrate 98g, Protein 77g.

41. SPICY CHICKEN SALAD WITH CRISPY TORTILLAS

Preparation Time: 15 Minutes

Cooking Time: 15 Minutes

Servings: 6

Ingredients:

- Chicken breast– 1lb / 454g
- Olive oil – 1 tablespoon
- Chicken seasoning - 2 tablespoon
- 2 Jalapeno peppers
- Low fat yogurt – 1/3 cup
- 6 Tortillas
- 1 Sliced mango

Instructions:

1. Take a bowl and add chicken strips, olive oil and chicken seasoning mix them well.
2. Add peppers as well and further mix them.
3. Now place the chicken pepper mixture in the basket (put some oil in the basket).
4. Select air crisp function then set the temperature to 400F / 204C and air fry for 8 minutes.
5. After that take them out and heat the tortillas as well.
6. Then add the chicken mixture, yogurt, cilantro and mango slices to the tortilla and serve.

Nutritional information per serving: Calories: 175, Fat: 5g, Carbohydrate 18g, Protein 20g.

42. SHREDDED CHICKEN WITH STEAMED RICE

Preparation Time: 5 Minutes

Cooking Time: 40 Minutes

Servings: 6

Ingredients:

- Olive oil – 1 tablespoon
- Rice – 1 cup
- Salt & pepper as required
- Powdered black pepper
- Smoked paprika - 1 teaspoon
- 2 Diced carrots
- 1 Diced bell pepper
- 3 Chicken breasts

- Chicken broth – 1 ¼ cup
- Chopped parsley
- ½ Chopped onion
- Minced garlic – 2 cloves
- Dried oregano – 1 teaspoon

Instructions:
1. Put the ninja foodi in saute mode and add oil and onion.
2. Then add garlic, paprika and oregano.
3. Cook for 5 minutes.
4. Include the rice and chicken broth.
5. Then put salt, pepper, carrots, bell pepper and chicken.
6. Now close the pressure cooking lid and select the pressure cooking mode.
7. Pressure cook for 8 minutes at "high" pressure.
8. After depressurizing open the lid and shred the chicken and serve with parsley.

Nutritional information per serving: Calories: 245, Fat: 7g, Sodium: 730mg, Fiber: 1.5g, Sugar: 0.8g, Carbohydrate 28g, Protein 17g.

43. TINY APPLE BITES

Preparation Time: 5 Minutes

Cooking Time: 15 Minutes

Servings: 5

Ingredients:

- 5 Tart shells
- Cinnamon – ½ teaspoon
- Nutmeg
- Ice cream
- Apple pie filling – 1cup

Instructions:

1. First you need to warm up the tart shells.
2. For that put the tarts in the cooking pot and select air crisp mode and set the temperature to 380F / 193C and cook for 4 minutes.
3. Till tarts are getting warmed up chop the apple slices in to small pieces.
4. Put the spices to the apple pie filling.
5. Now put the filling in to each and every tart shells.
6. Then take the rack and place it in the cooking pot and place the tarts on it.
7. Sprinkle the cinnamon over it.
8. Air fry the tarts at previous temperature for 5 minutes.
9. Take them out and let them cool.
10. Serve with ice cream.

Nutritional information per serving: Calories: 300, Fat: 12g, Sodium: 60mg, Fiber: 2g, Sugar: 15g, Carbohydrate 35g, Protein 6g.

44. TENDER CRISPED BURGER

Preparation Time: 5 Minutes

Cooking Time: 15 Minutes

Servings: 4

Ingredients:

- Ground chicken – 1lb / 454g
- 4 Cheese slices
- Salt & pepper
- 4 Burger buns

Instructions:

1. Cut the buns in half.
2. Create chicken in to patties.
3. Add salt & pepper as well.

4. Put the chicken patties to the basket and air crisp one side for 8 minutes at 375F / 191C.
5. Then take the patties out
6. Put cheese slices to the buns and put the patties as well.
7. Air fry the buns until the cheese melts.

Nutritional information per serving: Calories: 637, Fat: 37g, Sodium: 809mg, Carbohydrate 39g, Protein 35g.

45. TUNA CAKES

Preparation Time: 10 Minutes
Cooking Time: 10 Minutes
Servings: 5
Ingredients:

- Tuna - 2 packs (each 2.5oz / 70g)
- Breadcrumbs – ¼ cup
- Garlic powder – ½ teaspoon
- Powdered onion – ½ teaspoon
- Shredded Cheddar – 1 oz / 28g
- 1 Egg
- Chili sauce – 2 tablespoon
- Shredded Parmesan – 1 oz / 28g
- Paprika – 1 teaspoon

Instructions:
1. Take a bowl and mix all the things.
2. Divide the mixture in to 5 groups.
3. Crete patties from the hands and place in the ninja foodi basket.
4. Choose air crisp mode.
5. Set the time 10 minutes and cook at 400F / 204C.
6. Take out and serve.

Nutritional information per serving: Calories: 170, Fat: 6g, Carbohydrate 12g, Protein 17g.

46. TENDER CRISPED CHICKPEAS

Preparation Time: 5 Minutes

Cooking Time: 15 Minutes

Servings: 6

Ingredients:

- Chickpeas – 2 cups
- Powdered onion – ½ tsp
- Vegetable oil – 1 ½ tbsp
- Powdered black pepper – ½ tsp
- Turmeric powder - 2/8 tsp
- Powdered chili – ½ tsp
- Salt – ¾ tsp

Instructions:

1. Wash the chickpeas and dry them using a clean cloth.
2. Take a bowl and add chickpeas, oil and spices.
3. Then mix well them.
4. Put parchment paper in the ninja foodi basket.
5. Put the chickpea mixture in to basket and select air crisp mode then set the temperature to 400F / 204C.
6. Cook for 15 minutes.
7. Take them out and serve.

Nutritional information per serving: Calories: 60, Fat: 3g, Sodium: 312mg, Fiber: 3g, Sugar: 1g, Carbohydrate 8g, Protein 4g.

47. TASTY POTATO SLICES WITH SOUR CREAM

Preparation Time: 10 Minutes

Cooking Time: 20 Minutes

Servings: 8

Ingredients:

- Halved potatoes– 2lb / 907g
- Olive oil – 3 tbsp
- Powdered oregano – ½ tbsp
- Thyme – ½ tbsp
- Shredded parmesan cheese – 1/3 cup
- Minced garlic – 4 cloves
- Salt & pepper

Instructions:
1. Take bowl add potatoes, olive oil, salt, garlic, pepper, thyme, cheese and oregano.
2. Mix them well.
3. Put potatoes in to the ninja foodi basket. Do not over crowd. Do badges if it is too much.
4. Select air crisp mode and set the temperature at 400F / 204C.
5. Air fry for 10 minutes.
6. Stir the basket and make sure every side is equally fried.
7. Put the butter over it and serve.

Nutritional information per serving: Calories: 193, Fat: 11g, Sodium: 109mg, Fiber: 3g, Sugar: 1g, Carbohydrate 21g, Protein 4g.

48. TWISTED BREAD MIX

Preparation Time: 15 Minutes
Cooking Time: 15 Minutes
Servings: 3
Ingredients:

- Flour – 1cup
- Baking powder – 1 teaspoon
- Salt - ¼ teaspoon
- Garlic powder – ¼ teaspoon
- Light butter – 1 tablespoon
- Low fat yogurt – ½ cup
- Olive Oil (apply before cooking) – ½ tablespoon
- Olive Oil – ½ tablespoon
- Melted butter – ½ tablespoon
- Garlic powder – ½ teaspoon
- Shredded parmesan - 1 tablespoon

Instructions:

1. Take a bowl and add garlic powder, salt, baking powder and flour.
2. Well mix them.
3. Put the yogurt and butter then mix everything well.
4. Place the mixture on a cutting board and form a dough.
5. Separate the dough in to eight pieces.
6. Make eight strips from them.
7. Use two strips and twist them.

8. You have to make four twisted twists.
9. Then apply olive oil over the twists.
10. Choose air crisp mode.
11. Place them in the ninja foodi basket and set the temperature at 350F / 177C.
12. Cook for 15 minutes.
13. Till it is done, take bowl and put melted butter, ½ olive oil and garlic powder.
14. Take bread twists out and apply melted butter mix over them.
15. Sprinkle the cheese over it and serve.

Nutritional information per serving: Calories: 251, Fat: 10g, Carbohydrate 31g, Protein 10g.

49. TENDER BEANS WITH MELTED DRESSING

Preparation Time: 5 Minutes
Cooking Time: 25 Minutes
Servings: 8
Ingredients:

- Beans – 15oz / 425g
- Water – 4 cups
- Cumin – 1 teaspoon
- Salt – ½ teaspoon
- Garlic – 1 tablespoon
- Diced onion– 1 cup

Instructions:

1. Wash the beans from water.
2. Add beans to the cooking pot of ninja foodi.
3. Pour the water.
4. Close with the pressure cooking lid.
5. Select "high" pressure and set the time as 25 minutes.
6. This time use natural pressure release for 10 minutes.
7. Remove the remaining pressure from the pressure valve and open the lid.
8. Add the spices and serve.

Nutritional information per serving: Calories: 91, Fat: 1g, Sodium: 578mg, Fiber: 5g, Sugar: 1g, Carbohydrate 15g, Protein 6g.

50. TENDER CRISPED CORN

Preparation Time: 5 Minutes

Cooking Time: 35 Minutes

Servings: 4

Ingredients:

- Cornbread mix – 8 ½ oz / 241g
- Melted butter – ½ cup
- 2 Eggs
- Corn – 2 cans (15oz / 425g each)
- Sour cream – 1 cup

Instructions:

1. Take a bowl and mix all the ingredients.
2. Grease the cooking pot of the ninja foodi with cooking spray.

3. Put the mixture in to the pot.
4. Select air crisp function.
5. Close the air frying lid and set the temperature to 350F / 177C.
6. Cook for 35 minutes.
7. Let it cool and serve.

Nutritional information per serving: Calories: 312, Fat: 21g, Sodium: 382mg, Fiber: 1g, Sugar: 7g, Carbohydrate 25g, Protein 5g.

CHAPTER 8 – LUNCH RECIPES

1. ALL IN ONE SPECIAL CHICKEN

Preparation Time: 10 Minutes

Cooking Time: 20 Minutes

Servings: 4

Ingredients:

- Bacon – 10 stripes
- Ranch seasoning – 3 tablespoons
- Chicken broth – 1½ cups
- Cream cheese – 8oz / 227g
- Broccoli – 2 cups
- Shredded Cheese – ½ cup
- 5 Chicken thighs

Instructions:

1. Select saute mode and cook the bacon for 5 minutes and take them out.
2. Put chicken in to a bowl and add ranch seasoning.
3. Mix it well.
4. Then place in the ninja foodi cooking pot and select high heat under saute mode.
5. After that add bacon and chicken broth to the cooking pot.
6. Close the pressure cooking lid cook for 20 minutes in medium pressure.

7. Quick release the pressure (check chapter 3)
8. Then shred the chicken using a fork.
9. Same time cut broccoli in to small pieces.
10. Put the ninja foodi to saute mode again and add broccoli, cream cheese, and shredded cheese.
11. Mix everything well and let simmer for 5 minutes.

Nutritional information per serving: Calories: 320, Fat: 24g, Sodium: 462mg, Fiber: 0.4g, Sugar: 2g, Carbohydrate: 4g, Protein: 25g.

2. ASPARAGUS WITH WRAPPED BACONS

Preparation Time: 10 Minutes

Cooking Time: 10 Minutes

Servings: 5

Ingredients:

- Asparagus – 1lb / 454g
- Tomatoes – 2 cups
- Crushed garlic – 1 clove
- Salt – 1 teaspoon
- Olive oil spray
- Bacon – 10 slices
- Vinegar – 4 tablespoon
- Olive oil - 4 tablespoon

Instructions:

1. Apply olive oil over the basket of ninja foodi.
2. Take bowl and put oil, vinegar, salt and garlic. And mix well.
3. Take one asparagus and roll one bacon over it.
4. Place them inside the basket.
5. Put vegetables inside the basket as well.
6. Then coat olive oil and vinegar mixture over them.
7. Select air crisp mode and cook for 10 minutes at 400F / 204C.
8. Serve the dish.

Nutritional information per serving: Calories: 433, Fat: 10g, Sodium: 507mg, Fiber: 2g, Sugar: 4g, Carbohydrate: 8g, Protein: 35g.

3. BOILED EGGS

Preparation Time: 1 Minutes

Cooking Time: 15 Minutes

Servings: 3

Ingredients:

- 3 Eggs

Instructions:

1. Place the eggs in the ninja foodi basket.
2. Close the air fryer lid.
3. Select air crisp mode and cook for 15 minutes at 250F / 120C.
4. Once they are cooled remove the shell and serve.

Nutritional information per serving: Calories: 125, Fat: 8g, Sodium: 124mg, Carbohydrate: 1g, Protein: 12g.

4. BEEF STEW

Preparation Time: 12 Minutes
Cooking Time: 15 Minutes
Servings: 5
Ingredients:

- Beef – 2lb / 907g
- Olive oil – 1tbsp
- 12 Sliced mushrooms
- 3 Potatoes
- 2 Carrots – cut in to chunks
- Celery– 2 stalks
- Tomato paste – 3 tbsp
- Peas – ½ cup
- 2 onions
- Minced garlic – 3 cloves
- 2 bay leaves
- Dried thyme – ¼ tsp
- Salt & pepper

Instructions:

1. Take a bowl and put steak and season with salt and pepper.

2. Select saute mode in the ninja foodi and put the steak in to the cooking pot.
3. Cook both sides for 8 minutes.
4. Remove the steak and put onions, herbs and mushrooms to the cooking pot and saute them as well.
5. Then add remaining ingredients and water to the cooking pot.
6. Cut the steak and potatoes in to small cubes and put in to the pot.
7. Close pressure cooking lid and select pressure mode and cook for 5 minutes in high pressure.
8. Do a quick pressure release (refer chapter 3) and open the lid and serve.

Nutritional information per serving: Calories: 476, Fat: 11g, Sodium: 667mg, Fiber: 5g, Sugar: 7g, Carbohydrate: 25g, Protein: 35g.

5. BELL PEPPER SAUSAGE SALAD

Preparation Time: 5 Minutes

Cooking Time: 5 Hours

Servings: 7

Ingredients:

- Chopped tomatoes – 28oz / 794g
- Chicken broth – ¼ cup
- Salt – 1 tsp
- Oregano – ½ tsp
- Basil – ½ tsp
- Garlic powder – ½ tsp
- Red pepper flakes- ¼ tsp
- 1 Sliced bell pepper
- 1 Sliced onion
- Sausage – 7 links
- Powdered black pepper – 1 tsp
- Fennel seeds – 1 tsp

Instructions:

1. Add all the ingredient to the cooking pot.
2. Select slow cook function.
3. Close the pressure cooking lid.
4. Then select low pressure and cook for 5 hours.
5. Once it is done serve.

Nutritional information per serving: Calories: 615, Fat: 14g, Sodium: 1556mg, Fiber: 4g, Sugar: 8g, Carbohydrate: 43g, Protein: 25g.

6. CHICKEN FRIED RICE

Preparation Time: 10 Minutes

Cooking Time: 40 Minutes

Servings: 4

Ingredients:

- Chicken broth – 2 cups
- 4 Chicken thighs
- Rice – 2 cups

- 2 Sliced tomatoes
- 1 Sliced onion
- Minced garlic – 6 cloves
- 2 Chopped carrots
- Tomato paste – 1 tsp
- Soy sauce – 1 ½ tbsp
- Basil – ½ tsp
- Oregano – ½ tsp

Instructions:

1. Put olive oil to the cooking pot and select saute mode in your ninja foodi.
2. Then add chicken things and cook both side till they gain brown color.
3. Now take the chicken thighs and keep away.
4. Add onion and garlic to the pot and stir fry them for 1 minute.
5. Then add chicken broth to the pot.
6. Add fried chicken, carrots, rice to the pot.
7. Close the pressure cooking lid and cook for 8 minutes at high pressure.
8. Naturally release the pressure for 12 minutes.
9. Open the valve to release remaining pressure.
10. Then serve the dish.

Nutritional information per serving: Calories: 515, Fat: 15g, Sodium: 378mg, Fiber: 4g, Sugar: 6g, Carbohydrate: 70g, Protein: 26g.

7. CREAMY CHEESE SHRIMP CURRY

Preparation Time: 20 Minutes

Cooking Time: 10 Minutes

Servings: 8

Ingredients:

- Olive oil – 2 tbsp
- Diced onions – ½ cup
- Salt – 1 tsp
- Black pepper – ½ tsp
- Cream cheese – ½ cup
- Shrimp – 1lb / 454g
- Minced garlic – 2 tsp
- Rice – 1½ cups
- Chicken broth– 3 ½ cups

Instructions:

1. Put onions and olive oil to the cooking pot.
2. Select saute function and cook till onion gets tender.
3. After that add rice, garlic and keep cook in saute mode till rice is toasted.
4. Now add cheese, chicken broth, pepper and salt.
5. Mix well and close the pressure cooking lid.
6. Select pressure function and cook for 8 minutes at high pressure.
7. Do a quick release and open the lid. (Refer chapter 3).
8. Put shrimps to the pot and select saute mode again.

9. Cook till shrimp get tender.
10. Mix with the other mixture.
11. Then serve in a dish.

Nutritional information per serving: Calories: 637, Fat: 15g, Sodium: 2846mg, Fiber: 2g, Sugar: 5g, Carbohydrate: 65g, Protein: 44g.

8. EGG FRIED RICE

Preparation Time: 5 Minutes

Cooking Time: 20 Minutes

Servings: 5

Ingredients:

- Rice – 3 cup
- 3 Eggs
- Soy sauce - 5 tablespoons
- Vegetable oil - 1 teaspoon
- Chili sauce– 1 tablespoon
- Salt as required
- Chopped carrots and peas - 1 ½ cup
- 2 Sliced onions

- Sesame oil – 2 teaspoons

Instructions:
1. Take a bowl and put all the ingredients.
2. Mix them well.
3. Place it in the pan of your ninja foodi. (baking pan is ok)
4. Select air crisp mode and cook for 20 minutes.
5. Stir the rice few times while cooking.

Nutritional information per serving: Calories: 420, Fat: 3g, Sodium: 905mg, Fiber: 3g, Sugar: 2g, Carbohydrate: 78g, Protein: 15.

9. CRISPY PIE

Preparation Time: 20 Minutes

Cooking Time: 8 Minutes

Servings: 8

Ingredients:

- Ground beef – 1lb / 454g
- 1 Diced bell pepper
- Shredded cheese – ½ cup
- ½ of a diced onion
- 1 Egg
- Taco seasoning 1oz / 28g
- Water – ¼ cup
- 2 Pie crusts

Instructions:

1. Put your ninja foodi on saute mode and add peppers, beef and onions to the cooking pot.
2. Cook in high heat till beef gets light brown.
3. Add water and taco seasoning.
4. Stop saute function and let it cool.
5. Take the pie crust and unfold on a cutting board.
6. Cut 4 circles from one crust.
7. Take the remaining crust to make more circles.
8. You have to create eight circles.
9. Put the beef mixture in to the middle of the circle and roll out.
10. Add 2 tbsp to each circle.
11. Seal the edges using a fork.
12. Apply some oil in you ninja foodi basket.
13. Place the patties inside it.
14. Close the air fryer lid and select air crisp mode.
15. Cook at 350F / 177C for 8 minutes and serve.

Nutritional information per serving: Calories: 188, Fat: 15g, Sodium: 131mg, Fiber: 1g, Sugar: 2g, Carbohydrate: 2g, Protein: 14g.

10. CREAMY SPAGHETTI

Preparation Time: 15 Minutes
Cooking Time: 5 Minutes
Servings: 4
Ingredients:

- Ground beef - ½ lb / 227g
- Olive oil – 1 tablespoon
- Chili powder – ½ teaspoon
- Spaghetti - 1½ cup
- Beef broth – 1 cup
- Sour cream – ½ cup
- Shredded cheese – 1 cup
- Diced onion – ½ cup

- Salt – ½ teaspoon
- Diced tomatoes – 1 can

Instructions:

1. Put onion, olive oil, beef, salt and mix well.
2. Add in to the cooking pot and cook in saute mode till beef reduced pink color.
3. Stop the saute function.
4. Then add chili powder and tomato. Then further mix it.
5. Put the spaghetti to the pot.
6. Then add beef broth over it.
7. Close the pressure cooking lid and cook for 5 minutes in high pressure.
8. Do a quick pressure release (refer chapter 3)
9. Set back to the saute mode.
10. Add cheese and sour cream mix.
11. When the spaghetti becomes to the tenderness you want, stop the saute mode.
12. Now close the air frying lid and select air crisp mode
13. Then set the temperature to 400F / 204C and cook for 5 minutes.
14. Serve the spaghetti.

Nutritional information per serving: Calories: 487, Fat: 35g, Sodium: 1145mg, Fiber: 2g, Sugar: 6g, Carbohydrate: 25g, Protein: 20g.

11. CHILI DRUMSTICKS

Preparation Time: 5 Minutes

Cooking Time: 20 Minutes

Servings: 6

Ingredients:

- Chicken drumsticks – 1lb / 454g
- Coconut milk – 14oz / 397g
- Powdered Ginger – 1 teaspoon
- Garlic powder – 1 teaspoon
- Salt – ½ teaspoon
- Honey – 2 tablespoons
- Lemon juice - 2 tablespoons
- Paprika - 1 tablespoon

Instructions:

1. Take a bowl and put all the ingredients.
2. Mix well and let marinate for few minutes.
3. Put them in to the ninja foodi cooking pot.
4. Close the pressure cooking lid and select pressure function.
5. Pressure cook for 10 minutes at high pressure.
6. Do a quick pressure release (Check chapter 3).
7. Then put the ninja foodi in to saute mode and cook till you get the desired thickness.
8. Then turn off the saute mode and serve the dish.

Nutritional information per serving: Calories: 368, Fat: 32g, Sodium: 1536mg, Fiber: 12g, Sugar: 3g, Carbohydrate: 8g, Protein: 38g.

12. CHICKEN WITH CRISPY NACHOS

Preparation Time: 10 Minutes

Cooking Time: 30 Minutes

Servings: 6

Ingredients:

- Chicken Breast – 1½ lb / 680
- Beans – 15oz / 425g
- Chili sauce – ½ cup
- Water – 4oz / 113g
- Nachos – 6oz / 170g
- Ranch powder – 2 tablespoons

Instructions:

1. Add water, ranch powder, beans, and sauce to the cooking pot.
2. Close the pressure cooking lid and select pressure function and cook for 10 minutes at high pressure. Then do a quick pressure release. (Check chapter 3).
3. Then place the chicken in to a dish and shred using a fork.
4. After that select saute mode and cook in medium heat to reduce the liquid.
5. Then mix everything well.
6. Serve with nachos.

Nutritional information per serving: Calories: 296, Fat: 15g, Sodium: 323mg, Fiber: 3g, Sugar: 1g, Carbohydrate: 28g, Protein: 18g.

13. KAN KUN CHICKEN SALAD

Preparation Time: 15 Minutes
Cooking Time: 12 Minutes
Servings: 4
Ingredients:

- Powdered black pepper – ¼ tsp
- 5 Dried chili peppers
- Roasted peanuts – 2/3 cup
- 1 Chopped bell pepper
- Kan kun – 20oz / 567g
- 1 Chopped zucchini
- Salt – 1/8 tsp
- Chicken chunks – 1lb / 454g
- Olive oil– 2 tbsp

Instructions:

1. Put chicken in to a bowl and add salt and pepper.
2. Select saute mode and cook the chicken for 4 minutes in high heat.
3. Cook both sides.
4. Meanwhile take a bowl and mix other ingredients.
5. Then add them to the chicken.
6. Close the pressure cooking lid and select pressure mode and cook for 5 minutes in high pressure.
7. This time you can do a quick pressure release. (Refer chapter 3).

8. Serve the chicken salad.

Nutritional information per serving: Calories: 235, Fat: 18g, Fiber: 3g, Sugar: 2g, Carbohydrate: 29g, Protein: 34g.

14. CHICKEN POT CURRY AND RICE

Preparation Time: 15 Minutes

Cooking Time: 20 Minutes

Servings: 5

Ingredients:

- Diced bacon – 1lb / 454g
- 4 Chicken breasts sliced in half
- Cream cheese – 8oz / 227g

- Mayonnaise – ½ cup
- Shredded cheese – 2 cups
- 2 Chopped onion
- Chicken broth – ½ cup
- Cooked rice
- Ranch mix – 1 pack

Instructions:
1. Put the ninja foodi in to saute mode and put the bacon in to the pot.
2. Cook them till they become crispy.
3. Move the bacon in to dish when it is done. Stop the saute mode as well.
4. Now put the cream cheese and chicken inside the cooking pot.
5. Mix chicken broth in to pot as well.
6. Add ranch mix and close the pressure cooking lid.
7. Select pressure mode and cook for 15 minutes in high pressure.
8. Then do a natural pressure release for 5 minutes.
9. Remove the remaining pressure from pressure valve and open the lid.
10. Shed the chicken using a fork.
11. Select saute mode and put cheese and mayonnaise and mix well.
12. Add onion and bacon then mix further.
13. Serve the curry with rice.

Nutritional information per serving: Calories: 348, Fat: 24g, Sodium: 576mg, Carbohydrate: 1g, Protein: 30g.

15. CHEESY MACARONI

Preparation Time: 10 Minutes

Cooking Time: 25 Minutes

Servings: 5

Ingredients:

- Macaroni noodles – 1 ½ cups
- Water – 1 cup
- Salt – 1 teaspoon
- Pepper – ½ teaspoon

- Whipping cream – ½ cup
- Shredded cheese – 4oz / 113g

Instructions:
1. Take a bowl and put all the ingredients and mix well.
2. Take a pan which is comes with your ninja foodi.
3. Apply some oil over it.
4. Put the mixture over it.
5. Close the air fryer lid and select air crisp mode.
6. Cook for 20 minutes at 360F / 182C.
7. Serve the dish when it is cool enough.

Nutritional information per serving: Calories: 475, Fat: 30g, Sodium: 951mg, Fiber: 3g, Sugar: 1g, Carbohydrate: 32g, Protein: 22g.

16. CHICKEN SOUP

Preparation Time: 15 Minutes

Cooking Time: 5 Minutes

Servings: 6

Ingredients:

- Sliced chicken breast – 1lb / 454g
- Mixed vegetables – 1 can
- Olive oil – 1 tablespoon
- Whip cream – 1 cup
- Corn flour – 3 tablespoons
- Water – 3 tablespoons
- Salt – 1 teaspoon
- Minced garlic – 1 tablespoon

- Chicken broth – 1½ cup

Instructions:
1. Add the olive oil, chicken, garlic, salt in a bowl and mix well.
2. Put the mixture to the cooking pot of ninja foodi.
3. Select saute mode and cook till chicken losses its pink color.
4. Then add chicken broth and vegetables.
5. Mix well them.
6. Now close the pressure cooking lid and select pressure mode and cook for 2 minutes at high pressure.
7. Let the pressure release naturally for 5 minutes. Open the pressure valve before opening the lid to release remaining pressure.
8. Select saute mode again.
9. Now add whip cream, corn flour and water.
10. Pour it to the pot and mix well.
11. Stir well and put in to the keep warm mode.
12. Serve when you want.

Nutritional information per serving: Calories: 548, Fat: 33g, Sodium: 1429mg, Fiber: 2g, Sugar: 1g, Carbohydrate: 50g, Protein: 15g.

17. CUBED POTATO FRIES

Preparation Time: 15 Minutes

Cooking Time: 10 Minutes

Servings: 8

Ingredients:

- 8 Peeled potatoes
- Water – 1 cup
- Butter – 3 tablespoons
- Flour - 3 tablespoons
- Salt – ¼ teaspoon
- Milk – 2 ½ cups
- Chopped onion – ¼ cup
- Shredded cheese – 2 cups

- Pepper powder – ¼ teaspoon
- Cooking spray

Instructions:
1. Put some cooking spray in to the pot and add potatoes.
2. Then add water to the pot.
3. Cloe the pressure cooking lid and select pressure mode.
4. Cook for 1 minute at high pressure.
5. Release the pressure quickly. (Refer chapter 3).
6. Now take the cooking pan which comes with the ninja foodi.
7. Place it on the rack and put the potatoes on the pan.
8. Select saute mode and add butter.
9. Then cook in high heat.
10. Add flour, pepper, onions and salt.
11. Cook for another 12 seconds.
12. Now add milk and let boil for 60 seconds.
13. Then turn off the saute function and move in to a dish.
14. Then you can serve it.

Nutritional information per serving: Calories: 452, Fat: 10g, Sodium: 321mg, Fiber: 5g, Sugar: 4g, Carbohydrate: 62g, Protein: 15g.

18. CABBAGE BACON CASSEROLE

Preparation Time: 10 Minutes

Cooking Time: 15 Minutes

Servings: 3

Ingredients:

- Chopped beef – 1lb / 454g
- Sour cream – 4oz / 113g
- Paprika – 1 tablespoon
- Bacon - 3 strips (cut in to small pieces)
- Cheese - 5 slices
- ½ of a cabbage

Instructions:

1. Put beef to the cooking pot and select saute function.
2. Cook for 1 minutes in high heat.
3. Add bacon and paprika to the beef.
4. Stop saute mode when the beef get brown.
5. Then put the water to the pot.
6. Then add sour cream and cabbage then mix well.
7. Close the pressure cooking lid and select pressure mode and cook for 3 minutes at high pressure.
8. Then perform a quick release. (check chapter 3)
9. After that add cheese then serve.

Nutritional information per serving: Calories: 60, Fat: 2g, Sodium: 552mg, Fiber: 4g, Sugar: 0.5g, Carbohydrate: 10g, Protein: 4g.

19. FRIED RICE & PORK

Preparation Time: 20 Minutes
Cooking Time: 1 Hour 10 Minutes
Servings: 7
Ingredients:

- Kidney beans - 1lb / 454g
- Smoked pork - 1lb / 454g
- 1 Diced onion
- 3 Bay leaves
- Dried thyme – ½ tsp
- Oregano – ½ tsp
- Smoked paprika – 1 tsp
- Cayenne pepper – ¾ tsp
- Rice – 2 cups
- Fried sausages – 5 sticks
- Chicken broth – 4 cups
- Olive oil – 2 tbsp
- Soy sauce – 2 tbsp
- Minced garlic – 6 cloves
- 1 Diced bell pepper
- Diced celery – 2 ribs

Instructions:

1. First soak the beans for one night in water.

2. Put oil and sausages to the cooking pot and select saute mode.
3. Cook for 10 minutes at high heat.
4. Add onions and spices to the pot.
5. After some time add chicken broth and soy sauce.
6. Stir them well.
7. Then move the sausage mixture to a separate dish.
8. Put rice and beans to the pot.
9. Add some water and pork in to the pot.
10. Close the pressure cooking lid.
11. Select pressure mode and cook for 20 minutes at high pressure.
12. Let pressure release naturally for 15 minutes.
13. Release the pressure valve to remove the remaining pressure.
14. Shred the pork.
15. Mix everything well and serve.

Nutritional information per serving: Calories: 605, Fat: 43g, Sodium: 926mg, Fiber: 10g, Sugar: 5g, Carbohydrate: 42g, Protein: 40g.

20. FRIED PORK CHOPS

Preparation Time: 15 Minutes

Cooking Time: 1 Hour

Servings: 6

Ingredients:

- Pork chops – 5 pieces
- Flour – 1/3 cup
- Salt
- Powdered black pepper
- Olive oil – 1 tablespoon
- Heavy cream – ¼ cup
- Parmesan – ¼ cup
- Spinach – 2 cups

- Lime juice – ½ teaspoon
- Butter – 2 tablespoons
- Sliced mushrooms,– 8oz / 227g
- Minced garlic - 2 cloves
- Chicken broth – ¾ cup

Instructions:

1. Take a bowl and add pork, flour, salt and pepper.
2. Then mix them well.
3. Select saute mode in the ninja foodi.
4. Add some oil and add the pork mixture to the pot.
5. Cook each side for 3 minutes.
6. Take the pork out form the pot.
7. Add butter, mushrooms and cook 5 mins at high heat.
8. Then add garlic and chicken broth.
9. Further mix them.
10. Add cream cheese and parmesan to the pot.
11. Then put pork chops back to the pot.
12. Close the pressure cooking lid and cook for 10 minutes in high pressure.
13. After that do a quick pressure release.
14. Keep the pork chops on the rack.
15. Close the air fry lid and air fry for 5 minutes at 400F / 204C.
16. Mix spinach with the pork while it hot and serve.

Nutritional information per serving: Calories: 193, Fat: 12g, Sodium: 158mg, Carbohydrate: 3g, Protein: 23g.

21. FRIED HERB CHICKEN

Preparation Time: 1 Hour

Cooking Time: 35 Minutes

Servings: 8

Ingredients:

- Chicken – 2lb / 907g
- Thyme – 2 stalks
- Apple cider – 1 cup
- Sugar – 4 tablespoons
- Maple syrup – 4 tablespoons
- Thyme - 1 teaspoon
- Chopped rosemary - 1 teaspoon
- Water – 2 cups

- Salt - 1 teaspoon
- Black pepper powder – ¼ teaspoon
- 1 Chopped onion
- Garlic – 10 cloves

Instructions:

1. Take a large bowl and add all the ingredients (without thyme) and mix well.
2. Then put the chicken pieces in to it.
3. Keep it in the fridge for 30 minutes to marinate.
4. Then add thyme and put in to the cooking pot.
5. Close the pressure cooking lid and cook for 25 minutes in high pressure.
6. Quickly release the pressure after the time is completed. (Refer chapter 3).
7. Then remove the pressure cooking lid and close the air fryer lid.
8. Select the air crisp mode and cook for 10 minutes at 350F / 177C.
9. Open the lid and take the chicken out.
10. Serve to the table.

Nutritional information per serving: Calories: 1235, Fat: 65g, Sodium: 2635mg, Fiber: 12g, Sugar: 15g, Carbohydrate: 76g, Protein: 88g.

22. FRIED PRAWNS WITH DICED VEGGIES

Preparation Time: 5 Minutes

Cooking Time: 20 Minutes

Servings: 4

Ingredients:

- Prawns - 1½ cups
- Curry seasoning – 1 tablespoon
- Olive Oil
- Rice (cooked)
- Mixed vegetables – 2 cups

Instructions:

1. Put vegetable and prawns in to a bowl.
2. Mix well and move to the basket of ninja foodi.

3. Select air crisp mode.
4. Set the temperature to 360F / 182C and cook for 10 minutes.
5. Serve with rice.

Nutritional information per serving: Calories: 180, Fat: 5g, Sodium: 1210mg, Fiber: 2g, Carbohydrate: 18g, Protein: 12g.

23. FRIED VEGETABLES WITH SLICED BEEF

Preparation Time: 5 Minutes
Cooking Time: 15 Minutes
Servings: 6
Ingredients:
- Beef – 2 slices
- Chopped bell pepper – 1 ½ cup
- Diced Onion – ¼ cup
- Steak Seasoning – ½ tablespoon
- Cooking spray
- Diced pumpkin - 1 cup
- Sliced Mushroom, – 1 cup

Instructions:
1. Slice the beef in to small chunks.
2. Apply cooking spray in to the basket.
3. Move the beef and vegetable to the basket.
4. Mix with seasonings.

5. Apply cooking spray.
6. Select air crisp mode and cook for 10 minutes at 380F / 193C.
7. Serve them once they get cold.

Nutritional information per serving: Calories: 150, Fat: 3g, Sodium: 130mg, Fiber: 2g, Sugar: 3g, Carbohydrate: 7g, Protein: 10g.

24. HOT AND SWEET CHICKEN WITH BRUSSELS SPROUTS

Preparation Time: 10 Minutes

Cooking Time: 20 Minutes

Servings: 5

Ingredients:

- Brussels sprouts - 12oz / 340g
- Salt – 1 teaspoon
- Black pepper – 1 teaspoon
- Olive oil – 1 tablespoon

For chicken

- Diced Chicken - 1lb / 454g
- Olive oil – 1 tablespoon

- Chili powder – 1 teaspoon
- Salt – ½ teaspoon
- Chili sauce – 5 tablespoon
- Crushed ginger – 2 teaspoon
- Garlic powder – 1 teaspoon

Instructions:
1. Remove the stems of the brussels sprouts.
2. Put them to a bowl and add salt, olive oil and pepper.
3. Then place them in the ninja foodi basket and select air crisp mode.
4. Cook for 10 minutes at 250F / 120C
5. Then take a bowl and put chicken, oil, garlic, ginger, salt and chili powder.
6. Mix them well.
7. Then take the brussels sprouts and mix with chicken.
8. Add the mixture again to the basket and cook for another 10 minutes at 400F / 204C.
9. Serve with chili sauce.

Nutritional information per serving: Calories: 156, Fat: 5g, Carbohydrate: 6g, Protein: 20g.

25. HOT PEPPER BEEF

Preparation Time: 10 Minutes

Cooking Time: 20 Minutes

Servings: 4

Ingredients:

- Sesame oil - 2 tablespoons
- Minced garlic - 1 tablespoon
- Beef broth – ¾ cup
- Soy sauce – ¼ cup
- Pepper seeds – 1/8 cup
- 2 Chopped bell pepper (red/green)
- 7 Chopped onions
- Minced ginger - 1 tablespoon

- Seasoned beef with salt and pepper – 1½ lb / 680g

Instructions:
1. Put garlic, ginger and sesame oil to the cooking pot and select saute high mode.
2. Cook for 5 minutes and stop the saute mode.
3. Now mix the beef with it.
4. Include beef broth and soy sauce as well.
5. Close the pressure cooking lid and select pressure mode.
6. Cook for 15 minutes at high pressure.
7. When it is completed do a quick pressure release. (Refer chapter 3).
8. Then add pepper and onion to the pot.
9. Select saute mode again and combine beef and vegetables.
10. Cook for 5 minutes on saute mode.
11. Sprinkle some pepper seeds.
12. When you get the desired thickness stop the saute mode and serve in a dish.

Nutritional information per serving: Calories: 572, Fat: 30g, Sodium: 510mg, Fiber: 3g, Sugar: 4g, Carbohydrate: 22g, Protein: 51g.

26. HOME MADE MEATBALLS

Preparation Time: 15 Minutes

Cooking Time: 3 Hours 30 minutes

Servings: 15

Ingredients:

- Ground sausage – 2lb / 907g
- Pepper powder – ½ tsp
- Garlic powder – ¼ tsp
- Ground sausage – 12oz / 340g
- Breadcrumbs – 1 ¼ cups
- Shredded parmesan cheese – ¼ cup
- Salt – 2 tsp

Instructions:

1. Then put sausage, cheese, salt, breadcrumbs, garlic powder and pepper.
2. Well mix them.
3. Make balls from your hands.
4. Place them in the basket and close the air fryer lid.
5. Select air crisp mode and cook for 15 minutes at 380F / 193C.
6. Serve the dish.

Nutritional information per serving: Calories: 373, Fat: 18g, Sodium: 1605 mg, Fiber: 3g, Sugar: 8g, Carbohydrate: 22g, Protein: 31g.

27. MEATLOAF & STEAMED VEGETABLES

Preparation Time: 10 Minutes

Cooking Time: 1 Hour

Servings: 5

Ingredients:

- Roasted beef (seasoned with salt and pepper) - 2lb / 907g
- Minced garlic – 4 cloves
- Olive oil – 1tbsp
- Dried rosemary – 1 pinch
- Thyme – 1 pinch
- 2 Bay leaves
- Salt & pepper

- 8 Sliced mushrooms
- 2 Chopped carrots
- 3 Sliced potatoes
- 2 Sliced onions
- Beef stock – 1 cup
- Soy sauce – 1 tbsp
- Corn flour – 1 ½ tbsp
- Water – 2 tbsp

Instructions:
1. Put garlic and onion to the cooking pot.
2. Select the saute mode and cook till they become tender.
3. Add salt and pepper as required to your taste.
4. Then out mushrooms and stir cook.
5. After that put the beef stock to the cooking pot.
6. Include soy sauce, rosemary, thyme, bay leave to the pot.
7. Put the beef in to the pot.
8. Close the pressure cooking lid.
9. Cook for 45 minutes at high pressure.
10. Naturally release the pressure for 25 minutes.
11. Open the valve to get rid of remaining pressure.
12. Keep the beef aside.
13. Then add vegetables to the pot.
14. Pressure cook for 5 minutes at high pressure.
15. Again perform a quick release.

16. Take a bowl and add corn flour and water then mix well.
17. Mix the corn flour mix with the beef mixture and gain the thickness you want.
18. Serve the meatloaf with steamed vegetables.

Nutritional information per serving: Calories: 523, Fat: 28g, Sodium: 376mg, Fiber: 5g, Sugar: 4g, Carbohydrate: 24g, Protein: 50g.

28. NUTRITIOUS BEAN CASSEROLE

Preparation Time: 5 Minutes
Cooking Time: 15 Minutes
Servings: 8
Ingredients:

- Vegetable soup cream – 1 can
- Milk – ½ cup
- Black pepper – 1 teaspoon
- Fried onions – 1 1/3 cups
- Sliced beans - 4 Cups
- Salt – 1 teaspoon
- Cooking oil spray

Instructions:
1. Take a bowl and add soup cream, salt, beans, milk and pepper.
2. Mix them well.
3. Add fried onions as well.
4. Take the ninja foodi pan and put some oil and pit the mixture to it.
5. Keep the pan on the rack of ninja foodi.
6. Select air crisp mode and cook for 10 minutes at 350F / 177C.
7. Serve when it is done.

Nutritional information per serving: Calories: 137, Fat: 7g, Sodium: 793mg, Fiber: 3g, Sugar: 1g, Carbohydrate: 17g, Protein: 3g.

29. PASTA WITH BEEF

Preparation Time: 15 Minutes

Cooking Time: 20 Minutes

Servings: 7

Ingredients:

- Beef stew – 1lb / 454g
- Olive oil – 2 tablespoons
- Thyme – ½ teaspoon
- Flour – 2 tablespoons
- Beef broth – 4 cups
- Sour cream – ¾ cup
- Pasta – 10oz / 283g
- Chopped onion – ½ cup

- Salt – 1 teaspoon
- Sliced mushrooms – 2 cups
- Chili sauce – 2 tablespoons

Instructions:
1. Put oil, garlic, onion, mushrooms and salt to the ninja foodi.
2. Select saute mode and cook for 8 minutes.
3. Then add chili sauce, flour, thyme, and broth.
4. Mix them well.
5. Add pasta to the pot.
6. Close the pressure cooking lid.
7. Cook for 15 minutes at high pressure.
8. Do a natural pressure release. (wait for 5 minutes)
9. Release the pressure valve to remove remaining pressure.
10. Open the lid and put sour cream and mix well.
11. Serve the dish.

Nutritional information per serving: Calories: 395, Fat: 15g, Sodium: 981mg, Fiber: 2g, Sugar: 3g, Carbohydrate: 28g, Protein: 33g.

30. PORK POTATO TWIST

Preparation Time: 5 Minutes

Cooking Time: 25 Minutes

Servings: 2

Ingredients:

- 1 Potato (sliced)
- 6 Pork chops – 5oz / 142g each
- Olive oil – 2 tablespoons
- 1 Sliced apple
- Salt and pepper

Instructions:

1. Put the sweet potato in to a bowl.

2. Add spices (keep some for pork) and olive oil to it and mix well.
3. Place the potatoes in the basket.
4. Close the air fryer lid and cook for 15 minutes at 400F / 204C.
5. Remove the sweet potatoes from the basket.
6. Add asparagus, olive oil, salt and pepper to the basket and cook for 5 minutes at 400F / 204C.
7. Mix pork with salt and pepper.
8. Select air crisp mode and cook them at 325F / 178C for 8 minutes.
9. Serve potatoes and pork in a plate.

Nutritional information per serving: Calories: 495, Fat: 20g, Sodium: 735mg, Fiber: 7g, Sugar: 12g, Carbohydrate: 40g, Protein: 42g.

31. CHICKEN & SWEET POTATOES

Preparation Time: 10 Minutes
Cooking Time: 20 Minutes
Servings: 3
Ingredients:

- 1 Sweet potato
- Sliced chicken – 1lb / 454g
- Olive oil – 2 tablespoons
- Butter – 1 teaspoon
- Garlic salt – 2 teaspoons
- Pepper powder – 1 teaspoon

Instructions:

1. Put sweet potatoes in the basket and select air crisp mode
2. Then cook for 10 minutes at 350F / 178C.
3. Keep them aside.
4. Mix chicken, olive oil, butter, garlic salt and pepper in a bowl.
5. Place them in the basket and cook them for another 10 minutes at 380F / 193C.
6. Serve sweet potatoes and chicken together.

Nutritional information per serving Calories: 386, Fat: 15g, Sodium: 635mg, Fiber: 5g, Sugar: 7g, Carbohydrate: 38g, Protein: 39g.

32. PRESSURE COOKED SPINACH WITH SLICED PUMPKINS

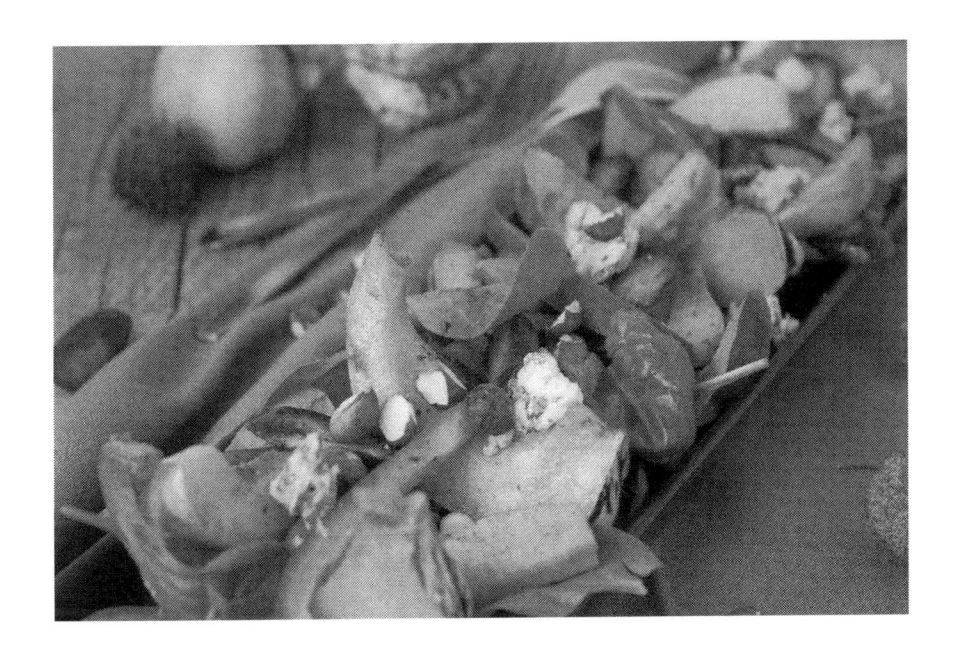

Preparation Time: 5 Minutes

Cooking Time: 20 Minutes

Servings: 8

Ingredients:

- Cream cheese – 8oz / 227g
- ½ a small pumpkin (sliced)
- Onion powder - ½ tsp
- Chopped garlic - ½ tsp
- Chilies
- Chicken broth – ½ cup
- Mozzarella cheese– 3 cups
- Shredded parmesan cheese – 1½ cups

- Spinach – 10oz / 283g
- Sour cream - ½ cup
- Salt - ½ tsp

Instructions:

1. Add spinach, sour cream, cheese, salt, garlic powder, mashed pumpkin, Onion powder, chilies and chicken broth to a bowl.
2. Mix well and close the pressure cooking lid.
3. Select high pressure and cook for 5 minutes.
4. Quickly release the pressure (refer chapter 3)
5. Serve the meal.

Nutritional information per serving: Calories: 364, Fat: 30g, Fiber: 1g, Carbohydrate: 7.5g, Protein: 17g.

33. PORK MACARONI

Preparation Time: 15 Minutes

Cooking Time: 1 Hour

Servings: 7

Ingredients:

- Roasted pork – 1lb / 454g
- Sliced garlic – 3 cloves
- Soy sauce
- Olive oil – 1 tbsp
- Salt – 1 tsp
- Mustard – ½ tsp
- Macaroni – 1lb / 454g
- Paprika – 1 tsp
- Chicken broth – 1 cup
- Paprika - ½ tsp
- 1 Sliced onion
- Chili sauce – 1tsp

Instructions:

1. Take a bowl and add salt, pepper and paprika.
2. Apply the mixture on the pork slice.
3. Then place the pork slice on the rack of ninja foodi.
4. Close the air fryer lid and select air crisp mode and cook for 7 minutes at 340F / 171C.
5. Till is done take another bowl and add soy sauce, chili sauce, mustard and chicken broth

6. Mix well and Put in the cooking pot.
7. Take the pork slice and shred using a fork.
8. Add them to the cooking pot as well.
9. Combine everything in the cooking pot.
10. Select saute mode cook till macaroni boils.
11. Also you can keep cooking till you get the required thickness.

Nutritional information per serving: Calories: 666, Fat: 12g, Sodium: 560mg, Fiber: 2g, Sugar: 4g, Carbohydrate: 54g, Protein: 42g.

34. PRESSURE COOKED TURKEY WITH NOODLES

Preparation Time: 20 Minutes

Cooking Time: 10 Minutes

Servings: 2

Ingredients:

- Noodles - 3oz / 85g
- Sesame oil – 1 teaspoon
- Chicken broth – 1½ cup
- Sliced bell pepper
- Chopped cilantro – ¼ cup
- Ground turkey – 8oz / 227g
- Pepper powder – 1 tsp
- Bread crumbs – ½ cup

- Minced garlic - 2 cloves
- Chopped scallions – ¼ cup
- 1 Egg

Instructions:

1. First prepare the noodles as mentioned in the packet.
2. Put the ninja foodi in to saute mode.
3. Add turkey, breadcrumbs, garlic, scallions, pepper and mix them.
4. Form patties from hand.
5. Select air crisp mode and close the air fryer lid.
6. Put patties in to the basket and cook them for 4 minutes at 380F / 193C.
7. Cook each side 2 minutes.
8. Add chicken broth the cooking pot.
9. Put noodles and patties in the pot.
10. Select saute mode and stir cook everything.
11. When the liquid is reduced serve the noodles in bowls.

Nutritional information per serving: Calories: 512, Fat: 15g, Sodium: 2703mg, Fiber: 2g, Sugar: 3g, Carbohydrate: 56g, Protein: 32g.

35. ROASTED BEEF & POTATO

Preparation Time: 10 Minutes

Cooking Time: 35 Minutes

Servings: 5

Ingredients:

- Sliced beef – 1lb / 227g
- Breadcrumbs – 1 cup
- 2 Eggs
- Salt and pepper – 1 teaspoon
- Soy sauce – ½ cup
- Chicken broth – 1 cup

- Diced onion – ½ cup
- 2 Diced potatoes
- Garlic powder – 2 teaspoons
- Dried parsley - 2 teaspoons

Instructions:
1. Put beef slices and all the ingredients to the cooking pot.
2. Keep mashed potatoes aside.
3. Then close the pressure cooking lid and cook for 20 minutes in high pressure.
4. Quick release the pressure and open the lid.
5. Select saute mode and cook till the liquid evaporates.
6. Then place the beef slices in the basket and close air fryer lid.
7. Select air crisp mode.
8. Cook at 340F / 170C for 15 minutes.
9. Serve mashed potatoes and beef slices.

Nutritional information per serving: Calories: 730, Fat: 24g, Sodium: 1514mg, Sugar: 18g, Carbohydrate: 82g, Protein: 45g.

36. ROAST CHICKEN BITES

Preparation Time: 10 Minutes

Cooking Time: 20 Minutes

Servings: 4

Ingredients:

- Chicken breast – 2lb / 907g
- BBQ Sauce – 1 cup
- Olive oil spray
- Flour – ½ cup

Instructions:

1. Slice the chicken nuggets in to small chops.
2. Apply flour over them.
3. Grease the ninja foodi basket with oil.
4. Choose air crisp function.
5. Place the chicken chops in the basket and cook for 8 minutes at 380F / 193C.
6. Apply sauce over them and air fry for another 3 minutes at same temperature.
7. Take them out and serve.

Nutritional information per serving: Calories: 443, Fat: 6g, Sodium: 775mg, Fiber: 2g, Sugar: 25g, Carbohydrate: 67g, Protein: 25g.

37. SLICED POTATOES WITH ROASTED BEEF

Preparation Time: 15 Minutes
Cooking Time: 30 Minutes
Servings: 6
Ingredients:
- Minced beef – 2lb / 907g
- 2 Eggs
- Oats – 2 cups
- Milk – ½ cup
- Sour cream – ¼ cup
- Butter – 4 tablespoon
- Corn – 12oz / 340g
- Tomato sauce – 1 tablespoon
- Chopped onion – ½ cup
- Salt – 1 tsp
- 3 Sliced potatoes - 3lb / 1.36kg
- Water – 1 cup
- Cream – 1 cup

Instructions:
1. Take a bowl and add beef, eggs, oats, milk, onion and salt.
2. Mix them well.
3. Then take an aluminum foil and put the beef mixture to it and cover the meat.
4. Keep it aside and cut the potatoes in to medium pieces.

5. Put the potatoes in to the ninja foodi and add water.
6. Keep the rack inside the ninja foodi.
7. Keep the wrapped beef on the rack.
8. Close the pressure cooking lid and cook for 25 minutes at high pressure.
9. After that quick release the pressure. (Check 3rd chapter).
10. Take the meat and potatoes outside.
11. Put potatoes in to another plate.
12. Take another bowl and put corn and butter and mix well.
13. Place corn on an aluminum foil as well.
14. Put the meat and corn on the rack again.
15. Choose the grill function and cook for 8 minutes at 400F / 204C.
16. Take them out and add salt and pepper.
17. Serve with potatoes.

Nutritional information per serving: Calories: 725, Fat: 31g, Sodium: 584mg, Fiber: 5g, Sugar: 15g, Carbohydrate: 75g, Protein: 36g.

38. SPAGETTI AND FRIED RIBS

Preparation Time: 10 Minutes

Cooking Time: 1 Hour

Servings: 6

Ingredients:

- Water – ½ cup
- 1 Back ribs
- Soy sauce - 2 Cups
- Cooking spray

Instructions:

1. Add water to the cooking pot.
2. Cut the ribs in to 3 parts.
3. Put cooking spray on the basket.
4. Apply soy sauce on ribs from a brush.
5. Put the pressure cooking lid
6. Cook in high pressure for 35 minutes.
7. Release the pressure quickly. (Refer chapter 3).
8. Then remove the pressure cooking lid and close the air fryer lid.
9. Select air crisp mode and cook for 15 minutes at 400F / 204C.
10. When it is done serve.

Nutritional information per serving: Calories: 331, Fat: 11g, Sodium: 1103mg, Fiber: 1g, Sugar: 12g, Carbohydrate: 41g, Protein: 14g.

39. SIMPLE RICE DIET

Preparation Time: 5 Minutes

Cooking Time: 3 Minutes

Servings: 2

Ingredients:

- Rice – 2 cups
- Water – 2 cups

Instructions:

1. Put rice and water in to the ninja foodi cooking pot.
2. Place the pressure cooking lid.
3. Cook for 3 minutes at high pressure.
4. Do a natural pressure release.
5. Open valve to get off remaining pressure if there's any.

6. Serve the rice.

Nutritional information per serving: Calories: 125, Fat: 1g, Sodium: 92mg, Sugar: 1g, Carbohydrate: 23g, Protein: 5g.

40. SWEET CHICKEN WING RICE

Preparation Time: 25 Minutes
Cooking Time: 20 Minutes
Servings: 8
Ingredients:

- Chicken wings – 2 ½ lb / 1.13kg
- Salt and pepper
- Minced garlic – 5 cloves
- Honey – ¼ cup
- Chili sauce – ½ teaspoon
- Grated ginger – ¼ teaspoon
- Paprika – 1/8 teaspoon
- Salt and pepper as required
- Baking powder – 2 teaspoons
- Cooking spray
- Butter – 2 tablespoons
- Cooked rice

Instructions:

1. Take a bowl and put chicken wings. Then and salt, baking powder and pepper and mix well.

2. Use the rack in your ninja foodi.
3. Place the wings on it.
4. Choose air fry mode and cook for 15 minutes at 400F / 204C.
5. Take chicken out.
6. Put butter, garlic, honey, chili sauce, paprika and ginger to the cooking pot.
7. Select saute mode and cook in medium heat till butter melts.
8. Then coat the chicken wings with the garlic honey mixture and serve with rice.

Nutritional information per serving: Calories: 241, Fat: 15g, Sodium: 120mg, Fiber: 1g, Sugar: 3g, Carbohydrate: 12g, Protein: 15g.

41. SAUSAGE VEGETABLE MIX

Preparation Time: 10 Minutes

Cooking Time: 20 Minutes

Servings: 6

Ingredients:

- Sausages – 5 links
- 2 Sliced bell pepper (red & green)
- Diced onion – ¼ cup
- Cajun Seasoning – ½ tablespoon

Instructions:

1. Put onion and pepper in the basket.
2. Place the sausage slices on the vegetables.
3. Sprinkle cajun seasoning on top of the vegetables.
4. Select air crisp mode and cook at 400F / 204C for 8 minutes.
5. Take them out and serve.

Nutritional information per serving: Calories: 165, Fat: 5g, Sodium: 841mg, Fiber: 2g, Sugar: 3g, Carbohydrate: 10g, Protein: 19g.

42. STEAMED PORK

Preparation Time: 5 Minutes

Cooking Time: 2 Hours

Servings: 6

Ingredients:

- Roasted pork – 2lb / 907g
- Water – 1 cup
- Salt – 2 teaspoon
- Black Pepper – 1 teaspoon
- Garlic powder - 1 teaspoon
- Pepper flakes – ½ teaspoon
- BBQ Sauce – ¾ cup

Instructions:

1. Add the water, roast pork and spices to the cooking pot.
2. Close the pressure cooking lid and cook for 10 minutes in high pressure.
3. Perform a quick pressure release. (Refer chapter 3).
4. Select saute mode in the ninja foodi and cook till the liquid evaporates.
5. Mix everything well and turn off the saute mode and serve.

Nutritional information per serving: Calories: 267, Fat: 8g, Sodium: 1073mg, Carbohydrate: 3g, Protein: 45g.

43. SPICY BEEF MIX

Preparation Time: 10 Minutes
Cooking Time: 10 Minutes
Servings: 4
Ingredients:

- Ground beef – 2lb / 907g
- Minced garlic – 1 teaspoon
- Olive oil – 1 teaspoon
- Chili powder – 3 tablespoons
- Cumin – 1 teaspoon
- 1 Diced tomato – 20oz / 567g
- Green chilies – 4oz / 113g

- Juice from 1 lemon
- 2 Bay leaves
- 1 Diced onion
- 1 Diced red pepper
- Salt – 1 teaspoon
- Smoked paprika – 1 teaspoon
- Cayenne pepper – ¼ teaspoon

Instructions:
1. Put onion, pepper and olive oil to the cooking pot and select saute mode.
2. And cook for 2 minutes in high heat.
3. Then add paprika, salt, beef, cayenne pepper, chili powder and cumin.
4. Stir cook. When the beef is brown stop saute mode.
5. Then add tomatoes, chilies and lemon juice.
6. Mix well and add bay leave.
7. Then close the pressure lid.
8. Cook for 5 minutes at high pressure.
9. Quickly release the pressure.
10. Serve the meal.

Nutritional information per serving: Calories: 260, Fat: 15g, Sodium: mg, Carbohydrate: 5g, Protein: 22g.

44. SWEET POTATO CHICKEN DISH

Preparation Time: 10 Minutes

Cooking Time: 7 Hours

Servings: 5

Ingredients:

- 6 Chicken thighs
- Water – ½ cup
- 2 Sliced sweet potatoes
- Ground cinnamon – 2 teaspoons
- Olive oil spray

Instructions:

1. Apply the olive oil spray in the cooking pot.
2. Put chicken in to pot.
3. Place sweet potatoes to the pot.
4. Sprinkle cinnamon.
5. Add water and mix well.
6. Close the pressure lid and select slow cook function.
7. Cook for 7 hours in low heat.
8. Serve when it is done.

Nutritional information per serving: Calories: 305, Fat: 11g, Sodium: 157mg, Fiber: 4g, Sugar: 3g, Carbohydrate: 12g, Protein: 35g.

45. STEAMED CHICKEN TORTILLAS

3

Preparation Time: 15 Minutes

Cooking Time: 10 Minutes

Servings: 5

Ingredients:

- Chicken breast – 1lb / 454g
- Olive oil – 2 tablespoons
- Chicken broth – 1 cup
- Corn– 1 can
- Black beans – 1can
- Rice – 1 cup
- Salsa – 2 cups
- Sour cream – 3 tablespoons

- Taco seasoning – ¼ cup
- Salt – ½ teaspoon
- 5 Tortillas

Instructions:
1. Pour olive oil to the cooking pot.
2. Put chicken to the pot.
3. Select saute mode and cook for 2 minutes.
4. Add the broth as well.
5. Put taco seasoning, salt and corn to the pot and mix well.
6. Add rice to the pot.
7. Place salsa on the top of them.
8. Close the pressure cooking lid and selects pressure mode.
9. Cook for 12 minutes in high pressure.
10. Shred the chicken.
11. Serve with tortillas.

Nutritional information per serving: Calories: 374, Fat: 12g, Sodium: 1165mg, Fiber: 8g, Sugar: 3g, Carbohydrate: 55g, Protein: 15g.

46. SHRIMP RICE

Preparation Time: 15 Minutes

Cooking Time: 10 Minutes

Servings: 4

Ingredients:

- Shrimp – 1lb / 454g
- 2 Sliced bell peppers
- Salt - 1 teaspoon
- Paprika – 1 teaspoon
- Garlic powder – 1 teaspoon
- ½ of a sliced onion
- Olive oil – 3 tablespoons
- Cooked rice

- Chili powder– ½ tablespoon
- Pepper – ¼ teaspoon
- Cumin – 1 ½ teaspoon

Instructions:
1. Take bowl put shrimps and olive oil then mix well.
2. Include all the other spices and mix well.
3. Now add bell pepper and onions.
4. Mix everything well.
5. Place the shrimps in the basket and close the air fryer lid.
6. Select air crisp mode and cook for 8 minutes at 380F / 193C.
7. Serve with cooked rice.

Nutritional information per serving: Calories: 415, Fat: 35g, Sodium: 678mg, Fiber: 2g, Sugar: 3g, Carbohydrate: 8g, Protein: 23g.

47. STEAK & BROCCOLI MIX

Preparation Time: 15 Minutes

Cooking Time: 10 Minutes

Servings: 5

Ingredients:

- Sliced steak – 1lb / 454g
- Minced ginger – 1 teaspoon
- Beef broth – ½ cup
- Sugar – 2 tablespoons
- Broccoli florets - 10oz / 283g
- Corn flour water mix - ¼ cup
- Minced garlic – 2 teaspoons
- Olive oil – 2 teaspoons

- Soy sauce – ½ cup

Instructions:

1. Put the garlic, ginger, steak and olive oil to the cooking pot.
2. Select saute mode in the ninja foodi.
3. Cook till meat turns in to light brown color.
4. Stop the saute function.
5. Mix soy sauce, broth and sugar.
6. Close the pressure cooking lid and cook for 5 minutes at high pressure.
7. Perform a quick pressure release and open the lid.
8. Put broccoli to the pot and select saute mode again.
9. Stir cook the mixture.
10. Now add the corn flour mixture and stir well until you get the desired thickness.
11. Serve with rice or noodles.

Nutritional information per serving: Calories: 189, Fat: 5g, Sodium: 1348mg, Sugar: 4g, Carbohydrate: 10g, Protein: 24g.

48. VEGETABLE NOODLES

Preparation Time: 1 Minutes

Cooking Time: 20 Minutes

Servings: 2

Ingredients:

- Rice noodles – 1 pack
- Water – 1 cup
- Mixed vegetables – 5oz / 150g
- Salt – ½ tsp
- Pepper as required

Instructions:

1. Add noodles and water to the cooking pot.
2. Include vegetables as well.

3. Mix salt and pepper also.
4. Close the pressure cooking lid.
5. Cook for 15 minutes at high pressure.
6. Then do a natural release for 5 minutes.
7. Let go the excess pressure by opening the pressure valve.
8. Serve the meal.

Nutritional information per serving: Calories: 346, Fat: 3g, Sodium: 8mg, Fiber: 3g, Carbohydrate: 75g, Protein: 7g.

49. VEGGIE & CHICKEN KABOBS

Preparation Time: 15 Minutes

Cooking Time: 20 Minutes

Servings: 6

Ingredients:

- 1 Sliced zucchini
- 1 Onion cut in to chops
- Diced chicken breast – 1lb / 454g
- Small tomatoes – 1½ cups
- Olive oil – ¼ cup
- Oregano – 1 teaspoon
- Olive oil spray
- Minced garlic – 1 clove

- Juice of 1 lime

Instructions:

1. Take a bowl and put garlic, lime juice, olive oil, oregano and chicken pieces.
2. Let the chicken marinate for 5 hours.
3. Take the skewers and put chicken and vegetables through them.
4. Then place them inside the basket and close the air fryer lid.
5. Select air crisp mode and cook for 15 minutes at 380F / 193C.
6. Serve them with sauce.

Nutritional information per serving: Calories: 212, Fat: 13g, Sodium: 95mg, Fiber: 1g, Sugar: 2g, Carbohydrate: 6g, Protein: 18g.

50. ZUCCHINI CUP CAKES

Preparation Time: 5 Minutes

Cooking Time: 8 Minutes

Servings: 6

Ingredients:

- 2 Zucchini
- Pizza sauce - ¼ cup
- Mozzarella cheese
- Olive oil spray
- Pepperoni

Instructions:

1. Slice the zucchini length wise.
2. Remove the middle seeds.
3. Apply some olive oil on zucchini.
4. Add peperoni, cheese and pizza sauce inside the zucchini slices.
5. Place them in the ninja foodi basket.
6. Select air crisp mode and cook for 8 minutes at 350F / 177C.
7. Once they are done serve.

Nutritional information per serving: Calories: 62, Sodium: 108mg, Carbohydrate: 5g, Protein: 1g.

CHAPTER 9 – DINNER RECIPES

1. AIR FRIED PIZZA

Preparation Time: 15 Minutes

Cooking Time: 20 Minutes

Servings: 4

Ingredients:

For dough

- Water – 2/3 cup
- Sugar – ½ tablespoon
- Salt – ½ teaspoon

- Liquid butter – 2 tablespoons
- Butter – 2 tablespoons
- Vegetable oil – 1 tablespoon
- Yeast – 1 ¼ teaspoons
- Flour – 1¾ cups
- Pizza sauce – 1 cup

For topping

- Olive oil – ¼ cup
- Feta cheese – 2 cups
- Any topping you like

Instructions:

1. Take a bowl and put water, yeast and sugar.
2. Mix well and keep aside for 10 minutes.
3. Put flour, salt, melted butter and yeast mixture to another bowl and mix with water.
4. Put the dough on a cutting board and mix well by your hands.
5. If the dough is sticky add flour and continue mixing.
6. Select the roast mode in your ninja foodi and preheat for 5 minutes at 390F / 198C.
7. Put the olive oil in the baking pan and place dough on it and make it a flat bread by hand.
8. Then apply some oil on the top of the bread as well.
9. Now close the air fry lid and set cook for 10 minutes.

10. When it's done, put some pizza sauce over it and put the desired topping you want.
11. Put some cheese as well.
12. Then bake for another 15 minutes.
13. Take it out and serve warm.

Nutritional information per serving: Calories: 718, Fat: 47g, Sodium: 1358mg, Fiber: 2g, Sugar: 5g, Carbohydrate 50g, Protein 23g.

2. AIR FRIED SHRIMPS

Preparation Time: 5 Minutes

Cooking Time: 20 Minutes

Servings: 2

Ingredients:

- 6 Shrimps – 1oz / 28g
- Powdered black pepper – ¼ tsp
- Lime zest – 1 tsp
- Diced garlic – ½ tsp
- Salt - 1/8 tsp
- Olive oil spray
- Diced parsley – 2 tbsp

Instructions:

1. Take a bowl and put cleaned shrimps salt and pepper.
2. Apply olive oil spray in the ninja foodi basket.
3. Put oil on shrimps as well.
4. Then place in the basket.
5. Select air crisp mode.
6. Cook for 5 minutes at 400F / 204C.
7. Take them out and put in to a bowl.
8. Add parsley, oil, lime zest and garlic then mix well and serve.

Nutritional information per serving: Calories: 348, Fat: 30g, Sodium: 650mg, Fiber: 0.5g, Sugar: 0.1g, Carbohydrate 4.8g, Protein 13g.

3. AIR FRIED PASTA COMBO

Preparation Time: 10 Minutes
Cooking Time: 7 Minutes
Servings: 4
Ingredients:

- Butterfly pasta – 15oz / 425g
- Butter – 1 tablespoon
- Minced garlic – 1 tablespoon
- Salt & pepper

Instructions:

1. Put some water to the ninja foodi basket and put the pasta to it.
2. Select saute option and cook for 10 – 15 minutes.
3. Take them out and drain water.
4. Put in to a bowl and add butter, garlic, salt and pepper.
5. Move in to the ninja foodi basket and choose air crisp mode and cook for 5 minutes at 350F / 177C.
6. Take out and serve.

Nutritional information per serving: Calories: 282, Fat: 23g, Sodium: 645mg, Fiber: 3g, Sugar: 1g, Carbohydrate: 35g, Protein: 12g.

4. AIR FRIED CHICKEN WRAPPERS

Preparation Time: 15 Minutes
Cooking Time: 8 Minutes
Servings: 3
Ingredients:

- 3 Tortillas
- Cooked chicken (shredded) – 3 cup
- Green chilies – 3oz / 85g
- Salt – 1 teaspoon
- Pepper – ½ teaspoon
- Shredded cheese – 1 cup

- Cream cheese – 3oz / 85g

Instructions:

1. Take bowl and add chicken, cream cheese, chilies, cheese, salt & pepper.
2. Mix them well.
3. Place ¼ tbsp of mixture to each tortilla.
4. Roll it and keep in the ninja foodi basket.
5. Select air crisp function.
6. Set the temperature to 360F / 182C and cook for 10 minutes.
7. Switch sides after 5 minutes.
8. Let it cool and serve.

Nutritional information per serving: Calories: 310, Fat: 22g, Sodium: 1145mg, Fiber: 2g, Sugar: 3g, Carbohydrate: 18g, Protein: 11g.

5. AIR FRIED POTATO CUBES

Preparation Time: 10 Minutes

Cooking Time: 20 Minutes

Servings: 6

Ingredients:

- 3 Diced sweet potatoes
- Honey – ¼ cup
- Olive oil – 4 tbsp
- Cinnamon – 2 tbsp
- Sugar – ½ cup

Instructions:

1. Put sweet potato pieces in to a bowl.
2. Mix with olive oil. Then add sugar, cinnamon and add honey.
3. Mix well everything.
4. Place them in the ninja foodi basket.
5. Choose air crisp function.
6. Set the temperature at 350F / 177C and cook for 20 minutes.
7. Once they are done let cool and serve.

Nutritional information per serving: Calories: 248, Fat: 7g, Sodium: 48mg, Fiber: 5g, Sugar: 1g, Carbohydrate: 47g, Protein: 1g.

6. BEEF KEBOBS

Preparation Time: 30 Minutes

Cooking Time: 10 Minutes

Servings: 4

Ingredients:

- Beef slices – 1lb / 454g
- 1 Green bell pepper
- ½ an onion
- 8 Skewers - 6 inches
- Sour cream – 1/3 cup
- Soy sauce – 2 tbsp

Instructions:
1. Put soy sauce and sour cream to a bowl and mix well.
2. Add the beef slices to the mixture and keep for 30 minutes.
3. Slice the bell pepper.
4. Now pierce the beef with a skewer and put peppers and onions to it.
5. Sprinkle some salt and pepper over it.
6. Select sir crisp mode and cook at 400F / 204C for 10 minutes.
7. Take them out serve.

Nutritional information per serving: Calories: 251, Fat: 15g, Sodium: 610mg, Sugar: 2g, Carbohydrate: 5g, Protein: 25g

7. BAKED CHEESE PASTA

Preparation Time: 7 Minutes
Cooking Time: 15 Minutes
Servings: 4
Ingredients:
- Pasta – 1lb / 454g
- Shredded cheese – 3 cups
- Salt and pepper
- Melted butter - ½ stick
- Breadcrumbs– 1 cup
- Bacon – ½ cup

- Chicken broth – 3 cups
- Water – 1 cup

Instructions:
1. Out the chicken broth and pasta to the ninja foodi cooking pot.
2. Close with the pressure lid and set "Low" pressure and set the time for 8 minutes.
3. Do a natural pressure release after 10 minutes.
4. Then remove the remaining pressure and open the lid and put cheese, pepper, salt and mix well.
5. Put melted butter and breadcrumbs to the pot and mix well.
6. Serve warm.

Nutritional information per serving: Calories: 265, Fat: 7.6g, Sodium: 518mg, Fiber: 2.4g, Sugar: 6.8g, Carbohydrate: 38g, Protein: 11g.

8. CHICKEN SOUP WITH BEANS AND CORN

Preparation Time: 5 Minutes

Cooking Time: 5 Minutes

Servings: 6

Ingredients:

- Diced chicken – 2 cups
- Taco seasoning packet
- Canned corn – 15oz/ 425g
- Water – 1 cup
- Pepper powder
- Beans – 15oz / 425g
- Sliced tomatoes – 14.5oz / 411g
- Chicken Broth – 14.5oz / 411g

Instructions:

1. Put all the ingredients to the ninja foodi cooking pot.
2. Close with the pressure cooking lid.
3. Select "high" pressure and cook for 5 minutes.
4. Go for a quick pressure release. (check chapter 3 for more)
5. Add the topping and serve.

Nutritional information per serving: Calories: 163, Fat: 1.3g, Sodium: 767mg, Fiber: 5.8g, Sugar: 1.8g, Carbohydrate: 26g, Protein: 12g.

9. CHEESY MACARONI

Preparation Time: 5 Minutes

Cooking Time: 20 Minutes

Servings: 8

Ingredients:

- Beef – 1lb / 454g
- Macaroni – 15oz / 425g
- Shredded Cheese – 4 cups
- Butter – 2 tablespoons
- Milk – ½ cup

- Sour cream – ½ cup
- Salt & pepper
- Water – 4 cups
- Sliced tomatoes – 1 can (15oz / 425g)
- Chopped chilies – 1 small can

Instructions:
1. Select the saute mode in your ninja foodi.
2. Place the beef in to the cooking pot and cook till it gets a brown color.
3. Add salt and pepper to the beef and mix well.
4. Stop the saute mode and add water, macaroni, chilies and tomatoes.
5. Now close with the pressure cooking lid and set pressure to "high" and cook for 5 minutes.
6. Do a quick pressure release and put cheese to the mixture.
7. Add milk, butter and sour cream.
8. Then mix well and serve.

Nutritional information per serving: Calories: 664, Fat: 38g, Sodium: 637mg, Fiber: 3g, Sugar: 2g, Carbohydrate: 40g, Protein: 34g.

10. CANNED BEEF WITH SHREDDED CABBAGE

Preparation Time: 15 Minutes

Cooking Time: 1 Hour 15 Minutes

Servings: 6

Ingredients:

- Canned beef – 3lb / 1.36kg
- 1 Sliced onion
- ½ of a cabbage
- 4 Sliced potatoes

Instructions:

1. Take bowl and put the beef and mix with the seasoning packet you get with it.
2. Now put some water in to the cooking pot.

3. Lace the beef mixture and the potato slices in the basket.
4. Choose pressure mode and set the pressure as "high" and cook for 1 hour.
5. Let pressure release naturally for 10 minutes. (Check chapter 3 for more information).
6. Release the remaining pressure.
7. Remove the basket and add sliced cabbage and onion to the cooking pot with juice.
8. Pressure cook them for another 3 minutes in "high" pressure.
9. Release pressure quickly.
10. Serve the cooked beef and potatoes with cabbage and onion.

Nutritional information per serving: Calories: 588, Fat: 28g, Sodium: 2355mg, Fiber: 6g, Sugar: 5g, Carbohydrate: 45g, Protein: 34g.

11. CAULI FLOWER SOUP

Preparation Time: 15 Minutes

Cooking Time: 30 Minutes

Servings: 5

Ingredients:

- Cauliflower - ½ lb / 227g
- Whip cream – 2 cups
- Corn flour – 2 tablespoons
- Diced cheese – 8oz / 227g
- Water - 3 cups
- 1 Diced carrot
- 1 Diced celery
- ½ a shredded onion

Instructions:

1. Chop carrots, broccoli, celery, and onion.
2. Then move them to the cooking pot.
3. Move the chopped vegetable mixture in to the basket and put diced cheese over it.
4. Take another bowl and water, flour and heavy cream.
5. Mix them well.
6. Pour in to the cooking pot.
7. Close the pressure cooking lid and choose "high" pressure and cook for 30 minutes.
8. Go for a quick pressure release and serve. (Check chapter 3)

Nutritional information per serving: Calories: 517, Fat: 42g, Sodium: 815mg, Fiber: 5g, Sugar: 4g, Carbohydrate: 20g, Protein: 18g.

12. CHICKEN & BACON FILLED JALAPENOS

Preparation Time: 10 Minutes

Cooking Time: 30 Minutes

Servings: 5

Ingredients:

- 3 Chicken breasts
- 5 Jalapeno peppers
- Powdered cumin – 1 tsp
- Salt & pepper
- 10 Bacon strips
- Cream cheese – ¾ cup
- Shredded cheese – ½ cup

Instructions:

1. Chop the chicken and put in to a bowl.
2. Add salt & pepper and cumin powder then mix well.
3. Include cheese to the mixture as well.
4. Remove the top and the seeds of the peppers.
5. Fill the mixture and the bacon to the pepper.
6. Sprinkle some cheese over the top and place in the ninja foodi rack.
7. Select air crisp mode.
8. Cook for 15 minutes at 400F / 204C.
9. Then serve them.

Nutritional information per serving: Calories: 286, Fat: 17g, Sodium: 428mg, Fiber: 3g, Carbohydrate: 6g, Protein: 56g.

13. CHICKEN STEW

Preparation Time: 10 Minutes

Cooking Time: 18 Minutes

Servings: 4

Ingredients:

- Chicken thighs – 1lb / 454g
- 2 Sliced bell peppers
- Olive oil – 2 tsp
- Chicken stew seasoning – 1 tbsp
- Salt
- 1 Diced onion

Instructions:

1. Take a bowl and add all the ingredients.

2. Mix them well.
3. Put the things in to the ninja foodi basket and select air crisp mode then cook for 15 minutes at 350F / 177C.
4. Serve with any topping you like.

Nutritional information per serving: Calories: 178, Fat: 5g, Sodium: 186mg, Fiber: 2g, Sugar: 3g, Carbohydrate: 8g, Protein: 24g.

14. CREAMY FISH

Preparation Time: 10 Minutes

Cooking Time: 28 Minutes

Servings: 2

Ingredients:

- Chicken broth – 3 cups
- 3 Small tilapia fish
- Heavy whip cream – 1 cup
- Butter – 2 tablespoon
- Salt – 1 teaspoon
- Fish seasoning - 2 teaspoon

- Vegetable oil spray

Instructions:
1. Put chicken broth, whip cream, salt, and butter to the ninja foodi cooking pot.
2. Close the pressure cooking lid and cook in "high" pressure for 8 minutes.
3. Wait for 10 minutes and naturally release the pressure. Open the pressure valve to remove the remaining pressure.
4. Remove the mixture to a dish.
5. Apply the fish seasoning over the fish and place on the rack of the ninja foodi.
6. Choose air crisp mode and cook for 10 minutes at 395F / 202C.
7. Serve the fish with the gravy.

Nutritional information per serving: Calories: 281, Fat: 13g, Sodium: 85mg, Carbohydrate: 14g, Protein: 41g.

15. CHEESY MACARONI & BACON

Preparation Time: 5 Minutes

Cooking Time: 15 Minutes

Servings: 14

Ingredients:

- Macaroni – 8oz / 227g
- 2 Bacon slices
- Milk – 1 cup
- Shredded cheese – 6oz / 170g
- Diced parmesan cheese – 1oz / 28g
- Minced garlic - 4 cloves
- Chicken Broth – 2 cups

Instructions:
1. Use the saute mode of your ninja foodi and cook the bacon slices in to crispy.
2. Take out the bacon and put garlic in the pot.
3. After that include the broth and then add macaroni.
4. Close the pressure cooking lid.
5. Set the pressure to "high" and cook for 3 minutes.
6. Perform a quick pressure release and add milk to the macaroni.
7. Then add the shredded cheese.
8. When cheese is melted add the bacon back to the pot and stir cook.
9. Add parmesan cheese as a topping and keep in heat for another 3 minutes and serve.

Nutritional information per serving: Calories: 120, Fat: 6g, Carbohydrate: 11g, Protein: 7g.

16. FRIED FISH WITH VEGETABLE SALAD

Preparation Time: 5 Minutes
Cooking Time: 12 Minutes
Servings: 4
Ingredients:

- Panko – ¾ cup
- Dressing mix – 1oz / 28g
- 2 Eggs
- 4 Salmon slices
- Lime wedges
- 1 Sliced zucchini
- 1 Sliced beans
- 1 Sliced carrot
- Vegetable oil – 1½ tbsp

Instructions:

1. Select the air crisp mode and pre heat the ninja foodi at 350F / 177C.
2. Take a bowl and put panko, dressing mix and mix well.
3. Put the egg to another bowl.
4. Then dip each fish slice in egg and then the panko mix.
5. Add vegetables in the basket as well.
6. Place them in your ninja foodi basket and spray some cooking oil.
7. Cook for 15 minutes and serve.

Nutritional information per serving: Calories: 314, Fat: 15g, Sodium: 223mg, Carbohydrate: 10g, Protein: 37g.

17. FISH LASAGNA

Preparation Time: 10 Minutes
Cooking Time: 40 Minutes
Servings: 4
Ingredients:
- 8 Lasagna sheets
- Mozzarella cheese – 2 cups

- Salt & pepper
- Grated parmesan cheese - ¼ cup
- Meat sauce – 3 cups
- Ricotta cheese mix

Instructions:
1. First brake the lasagna sheets in to pieces.
2. Take the ninja foodi baking pan and place the lasagna pieces in the bottom.
3. Then add a layer of meat sauce on sheets.
4. Add the ricotta cheese on meat sauce.
5. Put the mozzarella cheese over top.
6. Do the same process for twice.
7. Cover the pan with an aluminum paper.
8. Put 1 water cup to the cooking pot and place the baking pan over the rack.
9. Set the pressure as "high" and cook for 25 minutes.
10. Do a natural pressure release after 10 minutes. Check the red button and the display to make sure the internal pressure is normal.(Open the valve to release remaining pressure).
11. Now open the aluminum paper and sprinkle some cheese over it.
12. Then select air crisp option and set the temperature to 400F / 204C for 5 minutes.
13. Cut in to pieces and serve.

Nutritional information per serving: Calories: 475, Fat: 12g, Sodium: 1488mg, Fiber: 4g, Sugar: 7g, Carbohydrate: 43g, Protein: 26g.

18. FRIED ZUCCHINI

Preparation Time: 10 Minutes

Cooking Time: 15 Minutes

Servings: 5

Ingredients:

- 2 Sliced zucchinis
- Breadcrumbs – ¾ cup
- Salt – ½ teaspoon
- 1 Egg

- Cooking spray
- Garlic powder – ½ teaspoon

Instructions:
1. Put the egg to a bowl.
2. Mix breadcrumbs and seasoning in a plate.
3. Take a zucchini slice and dip in egg and breadcrumb mix.
4. Place them in the ninja foodi basket.
5. Spray some cooking oil over them.
6. Select air crisp mode and set the temperature to 340F / 171C and air fry for 15 minutes.
7. Fry both sides and serve.

Nutritional information per serving: Calories: 43, Fat: 1g, Sodium: 454mg, Fiber: 0.8g, Sugar: 1g, Carbohydrate: 8g, Protein: 3g.

19. FRIED SPICY CHICKEN KABOBS

Preparation Time: 10 Minutes

Cooking Time: 15 Minutes

Servings: 4

Ingredients:

- Chicken breast – 2lb / 907g
- Soy sauce– ½ cup
- Maple syrup – 3 tbsp
- Chili sauce – 2 tbsp
- Coconut milk – ¼ cup
- Green / red pepper if you like
- Lemon juice – 3 tbsp

Instructions:

1. Take bowl and mix soy sauce, lemon juice, coconut milk, syrup and chili sauce and mix well.
2. Place the chicken breast on it and let marinate.
3. Put the skewers through chicken.
4. Place them in the rack of the ninja foodi.
5. Select air crisp mode and cook at 355F / 179C for 15 minutes.
6. Let them cool and serve.

Nutritional information per serving: Calories: 362, Fat: 15g, Sodium: 1823mg, Fiber: 1g, Sugar: 7g, Carbohydrate: 19g, Protein: 46g.

20. GREEN ONION SOUP

Preparation Time: 10 Minutes

Cooking Time: 5 Minutes

Servings: 4

Ingredients:

- 3 Sliced onions
- Thyme – ¾ teaspoon
- Chicken broth – 30oz / 887ml
- Butter – 3 tablespoons
- Shredded cheese – ¾ cup
- Sliced bread
- Salt – ¾ teaspoon
- Hot chili sauce – 2 tablespoon

Instructions:

1. Put butter and onions to the ninja foodi cooking pot and use saute mode and fry the onions.
2. Put salt, chili sauce, chicken broth and thyme.
3. Close the pressure cooking lid and cook for 5 minutes at "high" pressure.
4. Release pressure quickly from the valve (Refer chapter 3 for more).
5. Serve the soup with bread slices.

Nutritional information per serving: Calories: 478, Fat: 15g, Sodium: 1987mg, Fiber: 4g, Sugar: 5g, Carbohydrate: 65g, Protein: 22g.

21. HOMEMADE YOGURT

Preparation Time: 10 Minutes

Cooking Time: 6 Hours

Servings: 12

Ingredients:

- Milk – 50oz / 1.4kg
- Greek yogurt – 2 tablespoon
- Vanilla – 1 tablespoon

Instructions:

1. Take a large mixing bowl and add milk and yogurt to it.
2. Mix well and pout it to the cooking pot.
3. Add vanilla as well.

4. Close the pressure cooking lid.
5. Don not seal the pressure valve.
6. Select slow cook mode.
7. Set the pressure to "normal" and cook for 6 hours.
8. In the ninja foodi deluxe there is an option called yogurt. So you can speed up the things with that.
9. After the 6 hours, Take it out and cover with a plastic wrapping paper.
10. Then keep refrigerated for 5 hours.
11. Take it out and enjoy it.

Nutritional information per serving: Calories: 81, Fat: 5g, Sodium: 56mg, Sugar: 5g, Carbohydrate: 7g, Protein: 4g.

22. HOT CHICKEN WRAPPER

Preparation Time: 15 Minutes
Cooking Time: 15 Minutes
Servings: 5
Ingredients:
- Chicken thighs (cut in to small chunks) – 1lb / 454g
- Cumin – 1 teaspoon
- Coriander – 1 teaspoon
- Salt – 1 teaspoon
- Allspice – ½ teaspoon
- Vegetable oil – 2 tablespoons

- Oregano – 2 teaspoons
- Cinnamon – 1 teaspoon
- Sliced Tomatoes – 1½ cup
- Cooked cauliflower rice – 1 cup
- Olives – 1 cup
- 1 Sliced cucumber
- Sliced lettuce – 2 cups

Instructions:

1. Take bowl and mix cinnamon, oregano, coriander, cumin, allspice and salt.
2. Add chicken and oil to the mixture and mix well.
3. Marinate for 30 minutes.
4. Place this chicken in the ninja foodi basket.
5. Select air crisp mode.
6. Cook at 355F / 179C for 15 minutes.
7. Shake the basket and fry every side.
8. Take a wrapper and put the chicken mixture cucumber slice, tomato slice, olive and lettuce.
9. Enjoy the chicken wrapper.

Nutritional information per serving: Calories: 315, Fat: 17g, Sodium: 1253mg, Fiber: 3g, Sugar: 5g, Carbohydrate: 12g, Protein: 30g.

23. HOT SPAGETTI & BEEF

Preparation Time: 10 Minutes

Cooking Time: 20 Minutes

Servings: 10

Ingredients:

- Salt – 1 teaspoon
- Black pepper – ½ teaspoon
- Diced tomatoes - 2 cans
- Beef broth – 2 cups
- Ground beef – 2lb / 907g
- 2 Diced onions

- Minced garlic – 6 cloves
- Chili Powder – 1 tablespoon
- Cumin – ½ tablespoon
- Chopped peppers - 7oz / 198g
- Tomato paste - 6oz / 170g
- Sliced Green Chiles – 4oz / 113g
- Spaghetti – 8oz / 227g

Instructions:

1. Put onion, beef, broth and spices to the cooking pot.
2. Close the ninja foodi with the pressure cooking lid.
3. Pressure cook for 8 minutes. Do a quick pressure release.
4. Then add tomatoes, chilies, peppers, tomato paste and stir well and add spaghetti.
5. Close the pressure cooking lid again cook for another 4 minutes.
6. Again do a quick pressure release let it cool and serve.

Nutritional information per serving: Calories: 324, Fat: 12g, Carbohydrate: 28g, Protein: 30g.

24. KETOGENIC CHICKEN SOUP

Preparation Time: 10 Minutes
Cooking Time: 30 Minutes
Servings: 7
Ingredients:

- Chicken breasts – 1½ lb / 680g
- Olive oil – 2 tablespoons
- ½ a chopped bell pepper
- Oregano – 1 teaspoon
- Ranch seasoning
- Cream cheese – 4oz / 113g
- Salt and pepper
- Chopped onion
- Minced garlic – 3 cloves
- Chicken broth – 5 cups
- Tomatoes – 10oz / 283g
- Butter – 2 tablespoons
- Chili powder – 2 teaspoons
- Cumin – 1 teaspoon

Instructions:
1. Put the ninja foodi to saute mode.
2. Put peppers, onion, olive oil and garlic.
3. Stir cook for 5 minutes.
4. Add the chicken broth to the pot.

5. Put all the other ingredients except cream cheese and ranch dressing.
6. Close the pressure cooking lid and set "high" pressure and cook for 15 minutes.
7. Do a quick pressure release.
8. Take the chicken out and shred using a fork and knife.
9. Put the shredded chicken back to the pot and add cream cheese and ranch dressing.
10. Saute for 5 minutes and serve.

Nutritional information per serving: Calories: 257, Fat: 15g, Sodium: 823mg, Fiber: 1g, Sugar: 0.5g, Carbohydrate: 6g, Protein: 23g.

25. LOW CARB HEALTHY PASTA

Preparation Time: 10 Minutes
Cooking Time: 15 Minutes
Servings: 6
Ingredients:

- Ground turkey – 1lb / 454g
- Chopped onion – ½ cup
- Italian seasoning – 1 teaspoon
- Spaghetti noodles – 1lb / 454g
- Diced tomatoes – 15oz / 425g
- Crushed tomatoes – 2 cans
- Water - 3 ½ cups

- Salt – ½ teaspoon
- Pepper powder – ½ teaspoon
- Garlic powder – 1 teaspoon

Instructions:
1. Select the saute mode of ninja foodi.
2. Put onions, ground turkey to the cooking pot and cook till meat gets brown.
3. Stop the saute and add water and put other ingredients and mix everything well.
4. Add noodles to the pot as well.
5. Then add tomatoes and two and half cups of water.
6. Put the pressure cooking lid and cook for 7 minutes at "high" pressure.
7. Quick release the pressure and open the lid (Refer chapter 3).
8. Let it cool and set. Then serve.

Nutritional information per serving: Calories: 527, Fat: 18g, Sodium: mg, Fiber: 5g, Sugar: 2g, Carbohydrate: 28g, Protein: 28g.

26. LIME MIXED TUNA SLICES

Preparation Time: 5 Minutes

Cooking Time: 45 Minutes

Servings: 4

Ingredients:

- Olive oil – ¼ cup
- Salt – 1 teaspoon
- Potatoes – 12oz / 340g
- 2 Zucchini
- 1 Medium pumpkin
- 1 Onion
- 1 Garlic
- Chicken breast – 15oz / 425g

- Rosemary - 8 sprigs
- 3 Limes
- Pepper – ½ teaspoon

Instructions:
1. Take a bowl and add pepper, salt, olive oil and potato cubes.
2. Mix them well.
3. Place them in the ninja foodi basket.
4. Select air crisp mode and cook at 425F / 218C for 10 minutes.
5. Till its done slice the pumpkin and zucchini.
6. Slice the onion as well.
7. Put them to a bowl and add salt and pepper. Then mix.
8. Cut the limes in to slices and keep aside.
9. Put chicken to another bowl and put oil and mix well.
10. When the potatoes are done turn the pieces the other side.
11. Now you have to make room for chicken as well as vegetables.
12. So divide the basket in to 3 sections and place chicken and vegetable on it.
13. Keep the lime slices on the chicken and whisk olive oil over the basket.
14. Set the temperature to 325F / 163C and cook for 20 minutes in air crisp mode.
15. Take the basket out and serve in a dish.

Nutritional information per serving: Calories: 346, Fat: 17g, Sodium: 740mg, Fiber: 3g, Sugar: 5g, Carbohydrate: 22g, Protein: 28g.

27. MIXED VEGETABLE BROTH

Preparation Time: 5 Minutes
Cooking Time: 10 Minutes
Servings: 10
Ingredients:
- Butter – ½ cup
- Flour - 6 tablespoons
- Pepper – ½ teaspoon
- Salt – 1 teaspoon

- Clam juice – 1 ¾ cups
- Water – 2 cups
- Dried thyme – 2 teaspoons
- Roasted garlic - 1 bulb
- Potatoes– 2 lb / 907g
- Olive oil – ½ teaspoon
- 1 Bay leaf
- Whipping cream – 1 cup
- Celery – 2 stalks
- 2 Sliced carrots
- ½ an onion

Instructions:

1. Select the ninja foodi's saute mode and put butter to it.
2. Then add salt, pepper and flour. Then mix well.
3. Turn off the saute mode and remove the mixture to another dish.
4. Put 2 tbsp butter, carrots, onions, celery and potatoes to the cooking pot and stir cook for 2 minutes under saute mode.
5. Then add water, thyme, bay leaf, ½ tsp salt, roasted garlic and mix well.
6. Add all the remaining ingredients and stir well.
7. Close the pressure cooking lid.
8. Set the "high" pressure and cook for 2 minutes. Do a quick pressure release and remove the remaining pressure from the valve and open the lid.

9. Remove the bay leaves. Select saute mode and select "high" heat and cook until the soup become thick.

Nutritional information per serving: Calories: 308, Fat: 18g, Sodium: 506mg, Fiber: 3g, Carbohydrate: 23g, Protein: 12g.

28. MIXED CHEESE SOUP

Preparation Time: 11 Minutes

Cooking Time: 5 Minutes

Servings: 8

Ingredients:

- Diced broccoli florets – 4 cups
- Cheddar cheese (shredded) – 3 cups
- Shredded cheese – ½ cup
- Shredded cooked chicken – 1 cup
- Butter – 2 tablespoons
- ⅓ Diced onion

- 2 ribs celery diced – 2 ribs
- 2 cloves garlic minced – 2 cloves
- Chicken broth – 2 cups
- Whip cream – 2/3 cups
- Cream cheese– 3oz / 85g
- Nutmeg – ½ teaspoon
- Salt – ¼ teaspoon
- Powdered black pepper – 1 teaspoon
- Cooked bacon – 4 slices

Instructions:
1. Put butter to the cooking pot of ninja foodi.
2. Select the saute mode and put normal "heat".
3. Then add celery, garlic and onions.
4. Stir cook for 5 minutes.
5. Include chicken broth, broccoli and cook till it starts to boil.
6. Close from the pressure cooking lid and set "high" pressure and cook for 5 minutes.
7. Let pressure release naturally for 10 minutes.
8. Remove the remaining pressure from the pressure valve and open the lid.
9. Now put cream cheese, salt, nutmeg, pepper and chicken.
10. Then mix them well.
11. Now select saute mode and let the soup boil.
12. Add cheese while mixing.

13. Then pour the soup in to bowls and serve.

Nutritional information per serving: Calories: 378, Fat: 28g, Sodium: 618mg, Fiber: 1g, Sugar: 3g, Carbohydrate: 5g, Protein: 23g.

29. MIXED SEAFOOD NOODLE FIESTA

Preparation Time: 15 Minutes

Cooking Time: 4 Minutes

Servings: 6

Ingredients:

- Salt – 1 teaspoon
- Pepper – ½ teaspoon

- Mayonnaise – ¾ cup
- Shrimp – 1lb / 454g
- Spaghetti noodles – 1lb /454g
- Chicken broth – 3 ½ cups
- Minced garlic – 1 tablespoon
- Sweet chili sauce – ¾ cup
- Olive oil - 1 tablespoon

Instructions:

1. Put the noodles in to the cooking pot.
2. Add the broth, olive oil, salt, garlic, shrimp and pepper.
3. Close the pressure cooking lid.
4. Pressure cook for 5 minutes at high pressure.
5. When time is up do a quick pressure release (check chapter 3) and open the lid.
6. Then add mayonnaise, sauce to the pot.
7. Mix well and take the noodles out and put in to a dish.
8. Sprinkle parmesan cheese when serving.

Nutritional information per serving: Calories: 618, Fat: 24g, Sodium: 2023mg, Fiber: 3g, Sugar: 18g, Carbohydrate: 75g, Protein: 25g.

30. NUTRITIOUS BEEF STEW

Preparation Time: 25 Minutes

Cooking Time: 35 Minutes

Servings: 6

Ingredients:

- Minced garlic – 2 cloves
- Chopped radishes – 8oz / 227g
- Beef stew – 3lb / 1.36kg
- Salt as required
- Powdered black pepper
- Olive oil – 2 tbsp

- Diced celery – 3 stalks
- 2 Sliced carrots
- Sliced mushrooms – 8oz / 227g
- Onion powder – 1 tbsp
- Italian seasoning – 1 tbsp
- Beef broth - 3 cups
- Parsley - ¼ stalk

Instructions:

1. Take a bowl and put beef and salt and pepper. Mix them well.
2. Put some olive oil to the cooking pot and add beef to it.
3. Select saute mode and cook till beef gets light brown color.
4. Put all the remaining ingredients, except parsley.
5. Mix well and close the pressure cooking lid.
6. Set the pressure to high and time as 35 minutes.
7. Once it is done do a natural pressure release. (Wait for 10 minutes. Remove the remaining pressure from the valve and open the lid).
8. Now add salt pepper to taste and sprinkle some parsley and serve.

Nutritional information per serving: Calories: 773, Fat: 50g, Sodium: 367mg, Fiber: 2g, Sugar: 2g, Carbohydrate: 8g, Protein: 63g.

31. PRESSURE COOKED SAUSAGE PASTA MIX

Preparation Time: 10 Minutes

Cooking Time: 5 Minutes

Servings: 5

Ingredients:

- Garlic salt – 1 teaspoon
- Basil – ½ teaspoon
- Water – 2 cups
- Cooked pasta – 2 cups
- Cheese – 1 cup
- Mozzarella cheese – 2 cups

- Spaghetti sauce – 24oz / 680g
- Powdered pepper – ¼ teaspoon
- Ground sausage – 1lb / 454g
- Olive oil – 2 tablespoon
- 1 Sliced onion
- Diced tomatoes – 1 can

Instructions:

1. Put sausage, onions, olive oil to the cooking pot select saute mode.
2. Cook till sausage becomes brown.
3. Now add the spices and mix well.
4. Put spaghetti sauce over the meat and mix well.
5. Add cooked pasta and mix well.
6. Pressure cook for 10 minutes in high pressure.
7. Use quick pressure release.
8. Add mozzarella cheese when the pasta is warm and mix and serve.

Nutritional information per serving: Calories: 573, Fat: 37g, Sodium: 1735mg, Fiber: 3g, Sugar: 5g, Carbohydrate: 26g, Protein: 28g.

32. PRESSURE COOKED RICE WITH FRIED CHICKEN

Preparation Time: 30 Minutes

Cooking Time: 30 Minutes

Servings: 4

Ingredients:
- 8 Chicken thighs
- Minced garlic – 4 cloves
- Tomato sauce – 1 tbsp
- Chopped parsley – 2 tbsp
- Dried oregano – 1 tsp
- Cooked rice – 1 cup
- Soy sauce – ½ cup
- Honey – 1 cup

Instructions:

1. Take a bowl and add garlic, tomato sauce, parsley, oregano and soy sauce.
2. Mix chicken with this mixture.
3. Marinate for 30 minutes.
4. Select air crisp mode in the ninja foodi and place the chicken pieces in the basket.
5. Cook at 400F / 204C for 10 minutes.
6. Take them out and serve with rice.

Nutritional information per serving: Calories: 360, Fat: 8g, Sodium: 1280mg, Fiber: 1g, Sugar: 17g, Carbohydrate: 22g, Protein: 46g.

33. POTATO BROTH

Preparation Time: 15 Minutes

Cooking Time: 40 Minutes

Servings: 5

Ingredients:

- Cooked bacon – 6 slices
- 1 Sliced onion
- Chopped celery – 2 stalks
- Chopped garlic – 3 cloves
- Milk – 1 cup
- Whip cream – ½ cup
- Corn flour – 2 tablespoon
- Toppings

- Cheddar cheese
- Green onions
- Salt – 2 teaspoons
- Ground pepper – ½ teaspoon
- Dried thyme - 1 teaspoon
- Sliced potatoes– 2lb / 907g
- Chicken broth – 4 cups

Instructions:

1. Select saute mode in your ninja foodi.
2. Put bacon in to the cooking pot and stir cook till they get crispy.
3. Remove the bacon and add some olive oil.
4. Now add celery, garlic, onion and seasonings.
5. Stir cook for 5 minutes.
6. Now put the chicken broth.
7. Stop the saute mode.
8. Add the potatoes. Close the pressure cooking lid.
9. Pressure cook for 10 minutes at "high" pressure.
10. Do a natural pressure release. Give it 10 minutes. Remove remaining pressure and open the lid.
11. Take a bowl and add milk and corn flour.
12. Mix the corn flour mix to the cooking pot.
13. Put the ninja foodi back to saute mode.
14. Stir time to time and cook for 5 minutes.

Nutritional information per serving: Calories: 564, Fat: 12g, Sodium: 2715mg, Fiber: 5g, Sugar: 4g, Carbohydrate: 58g, Protein: 23g.

34. PORK TACOS

Preparation Time: 10 Minutes

Cooking Time: 45 Minutes

Servings: 12

Ingredients:

- Pork – 4lb / 1.8kg
- Olive oil – 2 tablespoons
- Chili powder – ½ teaspoon
- Crushed oregano – ½ teaspoon

- Cumin – ½ teaspoon
- Corn Tortillas
- Diced onion
- Chopped cilantro
- Water – ½ cup
- Salt – ¼ teaspoon
- Powdered black pepper – ¼ teaspoon
- Garlic – 1 clove

Instructions:

1. First cut the pork in to small pieces.
2. Put the pork in to ninja foodi cooking pot and put in to the saute mode.
3. Let every side of meat fry.
4. Now add salt, garlic, pepper, chili powder, cumin, oregano and water to the pot.
5. Cloe the pressure cooking lid.
6. Pressure cook for 45 minutes at high pressure.
7. After cooking keep it for 15 minutes.
8. It will naturally release the pressure.
9. Remove the remaining pressure from the valve and open the lid.
10. Tear the meat from a fork and add them to tacos.
11. Then garnish with cilantro and onion and serve.

Nutritional information per serving: Calories: 470, Sodium: 159mg, Carbohydrate: 2g, Protein: 38g.

35. PRESSURE COOKED DEVILLED CHICKEN

Preparation Time: Minutes

Cooking Time: Minutes

Servings:

Ingredients:

- Chicken breasts – 1.3lb / 590g
- Chicken broth – 1 cup
- Diced tomatoes – 1 can
- Soy sauce – 1 tbsp
- Cumin powder – 1 tsp
- Dried oregano – 1 tsp
- Lemon juice – 2 tbsp
- 1 Sliced jalapeno
- Shredded cheese

- Salt – ½ tsp
- 1 Diced onion
- Chopped garlic – 6 cloves
- Diced cilantro – 1½ cup

Instructions:

1. Add chicken broth to the ninja foodi cooking pot.
2. Then add oregano, cumin, tomato, soy sauce, garlic, salt, lemon juice and put the chicken breast to it.
3. Let them marinate for 30 minutes.
4. Add the pressure cooking lid and cook 60 minutes under "high" pressure and do a natural pressure release for 10 minutes.
5. Remove remaining pressure from the valve and open the lid.
6. Now spread the cheese jalapeno pepper slices, onion slices over the top and serve.

Nutritional information per serving: Calories: 320, Fat: 3g, Sodium: 1135mg, Fiber: 4g, Sugar: 8g, Carbohydrate: 20g, Protein: 38g.

36. QUICK CHEESY BEEF SOUP

Preparation Time: 10 Minutes
Cooking Time: 20 Minutes
Servings: 8
Ingredients:

- Ground beef – 1lb / 454g
- Salt – ½ teaspoon
- Powdered pepper - ½ teaspoon
- 2 Diced onions
- Mustard – 1 tablespoon
- Chicken broth – 2 cups
- Low fat yogurt – 1 cup
- Powdered cheese – ½ cup
- 5 Sliced potatoes
- 3 Diced carrots
- Minced garlic – 4 cloves
- Chopped parsley – 2 tablespoons

Instructions:

1. Select saute option of the ninja foodi.
2. Put the beef in to the cooking pot and add salt & pepper and mix well.
3. When the beef get brown color, put potatoes, onion, carrots and garlic and mix and cook.
4. Then add parsley, chicken broth, mustard and further mix them.

5. Close the ninja foodi with the pressure cooking lid and cook for 10 minutes in "high" pressure.
6. Until the soup is done take a bowl and add cheese powder and yogurt.
7. Mix them well.
8. Now the pressure cooking should have done.
9. So do a quick pressure release and open the lid.
10. Add the cheese yogurt mixture over the top and close the normal lid again and set the "keep warm" mode. (Do not cook or start any operation, just close the lid to circulate the warmth of soup and blend flavors).
11. Serve after 5 minutes.

Nutritional information per serving: Calories: 190, Fat: 5g, Carbohydrate: 18g, Protein: 20g.

37. RICE AND BEEF PECCADILLO

Preparation Time: 5 Minutes

Cooking Time: 30 Minutes

Servings: 10

Ingredients:

- Ground beef – 2lbs / 907g
- Olive oil – 2 tablespoons
- 1 Sliced onion
- 1 Diced red bell pepper
- Minced garlic – 4 cloves
- Beef broth – 2 cups
- Cooked rice – 1 cup

Instructions:

1. Put some olive oil to the cooking pot and select the saute function "high" heat.
2. Add bell pepper and onion.
3. Then cook for 10 minutes.
4. Include garlic and cook for additional 1 minute.
5. Then add beef and cook till they become brown color.
6. After that add both and other remaining ingredients and close the pressure cooking lid.
7. Pressure cook for 10 minutes at "high" pressure.
8. Do a quick pressure release and serve with rice.

Nutritional information per serving: Calories: 203, Fat: 7.5g, Fiber: 1.8g, Sugar: 7g, Carbohydrate: 13g, Protein: 22g.

38. ROASTED BEEF WITH SLICED CARROTS

Preparation Time: 10 Minutes

Cooking Time: 1 Hour

Servings: 6

Ingredients:

- Olive oil – 1 tablespoon
- Potatoes (sliced) – 1lb / 454g
- Carrots (cubed) – 1lb / 454g
- Maple syrup – 1 cup
- Garlic Salt - 1 teaspoon
- Roasted beef – 3lb / 1.36kg
- Water – ½ cup

Instructions:

1. Put some olive oil the cooking pot of your ninja foodi and select saute option.
2. Heat up the roasted beef and make sure the both sides are equally roasted.
3. Then add water, carrots, potatoes, maple syrup and garlic salt.
4. Close the pressure cooking lid.
5. Pressure cook for 1 hour.
6. Let pressure release naturally for 15 minutes. And remove remaining pressure from the valve.
7. Now you can serve the dish.

Nutritional information per serving: Calories: 738, Fat: 38g, Sodium: 510mg, Fiber: 4g, Sugar: 35g, Carbohydrate: 60g, Protein: 58g.

39. RED CABBAGE SOUP

Preparation Time: 15 Minutes
Cooking Time: 12 Minutes
Servings: 5
Ingredients:

- Ground sausage – 1lb / 454g
- Chopped tomatoes - 1 can
- Beef broth – 4 cups
- Hot chili sauce – 1 tablespoon
- Rice (cooked) – 1 cup
- Shredded cabbage – 6 cups
- Olive oil – 2 tablespoon
- Diced onion – 1 cup
- Minced garlic – 1 tablespoon
- Spaghetti sauce - 24 oz / 680g

Instructions:

1. Set the ninja foodi to saute mode and add olive oil, onion, sausage, garlic, and cook until the sausage turns brown color.
2. Turn off the saute mode.
3. Then put the diced tomatoes, spaghetti sauce, broth and mix everything well.
4. Add the rice to the mixture.
5. Now add the cabbage leaves to the pot.

6. Put the pressure cooking lid and cook for 12 minutes at "high" pressure.
7. Then do a quick pressure release (refer chapter 3 for more information).
8. Serve the dish.

Nutritional information per serving: Calories: 409, Fat: 25g, Sodium: 1686mg, Fiber: 5g, Sugar: 10g, Carbohydrate: 28g, Protein: 17g.

40. SAUSAGE CHEESE LASAGNA

Preparation Time: 10 Minutes

Cooking Time: 15 Minutes

Servings: 5

Ingredients:

- Ground sausage - 1lb / 454g
- 1 Diced onion
- Grated parmesan cheese – ½ cup
- Olive oil – 2 tablespoons
- Lasagna sheets – 8oz / 227g
- Spaghetti sauce - 24oz / 680g
- Water – 2 cups
- Garlic salt - ¼ teaspoon

- Salt - ¼ teaspoon
- Mozzarella cheese – 1 ½ cup

Instructions:

1. Select the saute option and add onions, olive oil, and ground sausage, salt and stir cook till sausage turn in to light brown color.
2. Take the mixture out and put in to bowl,
3. Now take ninja foodi baking pan.
4. Apply some oil over it.
5. Now place the lasagna sheets over the bottom layer.
6. Then add a layer of sausage mixture over it
7. Then add the spaghetti sauce.
8. Again put a layer of lasagna sheets.
9. Then add final layer of sausage mixture and spaghetti sauce,
10. Then put the lasagna sheets.
11. Add mozzarella cheese and parmesan cheese over the top and place on the ninja foodi rack.
12. Select air crisp mode and cook for 15 minutes at 400F / 204C.
13. When the cheese is melted you can enjoy the sausage lasagna.

Nutritional information per serving: Calories: 333, Fat: 15g, Sodium: 1105mg, Fiber: 3g, Sugar: 8g, Carbohydrate: 38g, Protein: 15g.

41. SPICY BEEF STEW

Preparation Time: 10 Minutes
Cooking Time: 30 Minutes
Servings: 6
Ingredients:

- Beef – 1½ lb / 680g
- Diced onion – ½ cup
- Beef broth – 3 cups
- Garlic powder - 2 cloves
- Hot sauce – 2 teaspoons
- 3 Diced potatoes
- 2 Sliced carrots
- Diced celery - 2 stalks
- Corn flour – 2 tablespoons
- 1 Bay leaf
- Paprika – 2 teaspoons
- Cooking spray

Instructions:

1. Add some cooking onion, beef and cooking spray then set the ninja foodi to saute mode and fry and stir them.
2. Then include paprika, broth, garlic, bay leaf, hot sauce, carrots, potatoes and celery.
3. Close the pressure cooking lid and cook for 30 minutes under "high" pressure.

4. Naturally release the pressure for 1o minutes. Remove the remaining pressure via pressure valve.
5. Let it cool and enjoy the dish.

Nutritional information per serving: Calories: 625, Fat: 15g, Sodium: 1135mg, Fiber: 5g, Sugar: 4g, Carbohydrate: 40g, Protein: 80g.

42. STIR FRIED CARROTS

Preparation Time: 15 Minutes

Cooking Time: 12 Minutes

Servings: 5

Ingredients:

- Sliced carrots – 1½ lb / 680g
- Onion powder - 2 teaspoons
- Thyme - 2 teaspoons
- Parmesan cheese
- Pepper & salt
- Olive oil – 3 tablespoons
- Wheat flour – ¾ cup
- Garlic powder - 2 teaspoons

Instructions:

1. Put carrot slices in to the bowl and mix with oil.
2. Add salt, flour, garlic powder, onion, thyme and mix well.
3. Take carrots and roll on the flour mixture.
4. Select air crisp function.
5. Place the carrots in the basket and set the temperature at 390F / 198C and air fry for 12 minutes.
6. Serve with cheese.

Nutritional information per serving: Calories: 172, Fat: 7g, Sodium: 468mg, Fiber: 4g, Sugar: 5g, Carbohydrate: 25g, Protein: 3g.

43. STEAMED BEANS WITH MASHED POTATOES

Preparation Time: 10 Minutes

Cooking Time: 6 Hours

Servings: 8

Ingredients:

- 6 Mashed potatoes
- Beans – 2lb / 907g
- Diced onion – ¼ cup
- Chopped dill – ¼ cup
- Water – 4 cups
- Salt & pepper
- Bacon – 2 slices

Instructions:

1. Take a bowl and add all the ingredients.
2. Put the mixture to the ninja foodi basket.
3. Choose air crisp mode.
4. Set the temperature at 400F / 204C and air fry for 10 minutes.
5. Let it cool and serve.

Nutritional information per serving: Calories: 254, Fat: 3g, Sodium: 156mg, Fiber: 9g, Sugar: 8g, Carbohydrate: 54g, Protein: 7g.

44. SMOOTH LASAGNA

Preparation Time: 10 Minutes
Cooking Time: 30 Minutes
Servings: 8
Ingredients:

- Ground beef – 1lb / 454g
- Meat sauce – 25oz / 708g
- Dried basil - 1 Teaspoon
- Water – 6 cups
- Lasagna sheets – 12oz / 340g
- Mozzarella cheese – 1cup
- Spinach – 1cup

- Garlic (crushed) – 1 clove

Instructions:

1. Put beef to the cooking pot and use the saute mode and cook till beef gets light brown color.
2. After that add water, spinach, basil, sauce and garlic.
3. Close with the pressure cooking lid and cook at "high" pressure for 5 minutes.
4. Then take the baking pan and add lasagna cheese to the bottom.
5. Then add the beef mixture. Then sheets. Do this till you fish the mixture as well as lasagna sheets.
6. Sprinkle some cheese over the top.
7. Cover the pan with an aluminum paper.
8. Select air crisp mode and air fry for 30 minutes at 310F / 154C.
9. When the cheese is melted take it out.
10. Let it cool and serve.

Nutritional information per serving: Calories: 304, Fat: 12g, Sodium: 462mg, Fiber: 4g, Sugar: 8g, Carbohydrate: 25g, Protein: 24g.

45. SLICED BEEF WITH CHIPS

Preparation Time: 10 Minutes

Cooking Time: 2 Hours 30 Minutes

Servings: 6

Ingredients:

- Roasted beef – 2lb / 907g
- Oregano (dried) – 2 teaspoons
- Cumin – 1 teaspoon
- Sugar – 2 teaspoons
- Salt – 1 ½ teaspoons
- Chili powder - 1 teaspoon
- Garlic powder – 1 teaspoon
- Vegetable oil – 1 teaspoon
- 1 Sliced onion

- Potato chips – 1 pack

Instructions:
1. Take a bowl and add sugar, oregano, chili powder, salt, garlic powder, cumin and mix well.
2. Add some oil to the cooking pot and add beef to it.
3. Select saute mode with high heat.
4. Cook for 3 minutes till it gets fried.
5. Add the garlic powder mix and onion slices to the beef and mix well.
6. Move the beef mixture to the basket and fill the cooking pot with 2 cups of water.
7. Close the pressure cooking lid and cook for 10 minutes at high pressure.
8. Remove the water and cover the basket with an aluminum paper.
9. Select air crisp function.
10. Set the temperature to 350F / 177C cook for 10 minutes.
11. Enjoy with chips.

Nutritional information per serving: Calories: 301, Fat: 15g, Sodium: 1856mg, Fiber: 1g, Carbohydrate: 23g, Protein: 20g.

46. SIMPLE DHAL SOUP

Preparation Time: 10 Minutes

Cooking Time: 40 Minutes

Servings: 4

Ingredients:

- 1 Chopped onion
- 1 Chopped carrot
- Diced celery – 2 stalks
- Salt & pepper to taste
- Vegetable broth – 4 cups
- Spinach – 4 cups

- Grated cheese
- Minced garlic - 3 cloves
- Dhal – 1½ cups
- Diced tomatoes – 1 can

Instructions:

1. Add onion, garlic, celery, carrot, dhal and tomatoes to the cooking pot.
2. Put some salt and pepper.
3. Then add the broth and close with the pressure cooking lid.
4. Set high pressure and cook for 19 minutes.
5. Once it is done do a natural pressure release. Then remove the remaining pressure from valve and open the lid.
6. Serve with spinach and cheese.

Nutritional information per serving: Calories: 58, Fat: 1g, Sodium: 533mg, Carbohydrate: 8g, Protein: 4g.

47. SAUSAGE MIXED CORN SOUP

Preparation Time: 15 Minutes
Cooking Time: 10 Minutes
Servings: 5
Ingredients:

- Sausages – 1lb / 454g
- ½ a diced onion
- Beans – 14oz / 397g
- Dried oregano – 1 teaspoon
- Salt – ¼ teaspoon
- Kale – 3 cups
- Water – 6 cups
- Chicken broth – 2 cups
- Chopped tomatoes – 27oz / 765g
- Minced garlic – 1 tablespoon

Instructions:

1. Soak the beans in a bowl of water over night.
2. Add olive oil, sausages and onions to the cooking pot and cook in saute mode with high heat until onion and sausages get fried.
3. Putt all spices and mix sausage and onion with them.
4. Add tomatoes, beans, chicken broth and mix well.
5. Close the pressure cooking lid.
6. Cook at high pressure for 10 minutes.
7. Then do a quick pressure release and serve.

Nutritional information per serving: Calories: 430, Fat: 23g, Sodium: 1505mg, Fiber: 7g, Sugar: 5g, Carbohydrate: 30g, Protein: 24g.

48. TURKEY WITH GRREN BEANS

Preparation Time: 10 Minutes
Cooking Time: 10 Minutes
Servings: 4
Ingredients:
- Turkey (shredded) – 2 cups
- Turkey stuffing – 1 pack
- Green beans – 15oz / 425g
- Turkey gravy - 15oz / 425g
- Water – 2 ½ cups

Instructions:
1. Add water cup to the cooking pot.
2. Take the ninja foodi baking pan and apply olive oil over it.
3. Put the turkey in to the dish.
4. Add the stuffing and top with green beans.
5. Put a gravy layer over it.
6. Place the baking pan on the rack.
7. Pressure cook for 10 minutes at high pressure. (close with pressure cooking lid)
8. Go for a quick pressure release and open the lid.

9. Let it cool for 8 minutes.
10. Then serve the dish.

Nutritional information per serving: Calories: 322, Fat: 5g, Sodium: 905mg, Fiber: 4g, Sugar: 6g, Carbohydrate: 24g, Protein: 26g.

49. TURKEY STOCK

Preparation Time: 10 Minutes
Cooking Time: 25 Minutes
Servings: 5
Ingredients:

- 3 Turkey thighs
- Asparagus – 1 stalk
- Turkey broth – 1½ cup
- Pesto sauce – 6oz / 170g
- Tomatoes – 1 cup

Instructions:

1. Place the chicken layer at the bottom of cooking pot.
2. Then put the vegetable layer.
3. Again put the chicken layer.
4. Now pour the chicken broth over the chicken and vegetables.
5. Add the pesto sauce on the top as well.

6. Close the pressure cooking lid and cook for 25 minutes at high pressure.
7. This time do a quick pressure release and open the lid and serve when it is cool down.

Nutritional information per serving: Calories: 318, Fat: 23g, Sodium: 324mg, Fiber: 1g, Sugar: 3g, Carbohydrate: 10g, Protein: 25g.

50. TENDER CRISPED TURKEY

Preparation Time: 15 Minutes

Cooking Time: 40 Minutes

Servings: 5

Ingredients:

- Sliced turkey breast – 4lb / 1.8kg
- 1 Sliced onion
- Oregano – ½ teaspoon
- Garlic powder – 1½ teaspoon
- Onion powder – ½ teaspoon
- Salt – ¼ teaspoon
- Pepper – 1/8 teaspoon
- Olive oil – 3 tablespoon
- 2 Sliced potatoes
- Chicken broth – ½ cup

- Thyme – ½ teaspoon

Instructions:

1. Place a layer of potatoes in the cooking pot.
2. Then sprinkle the onion slices over them.
3. Take a bowl and add turkey, oregano, thyme, garlic powder, salt, onion powder and pepper.
4. Mix them well.
5. Put the turkey breast over the potatoes.
6. Add the broth around the turkey
7. Now add the turkey mixture in to cooking pot with potatoes and onions.
8. Close the pressure cooking lid and cook for 35 minutes at high pressure.
9. Then remove the pressure cooking lid.
10. Then choose air crisp mode and close the air frying lid.
11. Set the temperature to 350F / 176C and air fry for 15 minutes.
12. Then take it out and let cool and serve in a dish.

Nutritional information per serving: Calories: 245, Fat: 10g, Sodium: 976mg, Fiber: 2g, Carbohydrate: 12g, Protein: 31g.

CHAPTER 10 – DESSERT RECIPES

1. AIR FRIED FRITTERS

Preparation Time: 10 Minutes

Cooking Time: 5 Minutes

Servings: 3

Ingredients:

- 1 Tin of flakey biscuits -15oz / 425g
- Sugar powder – ½ cup
- Milk – 1 tablespoon
- 1 Diced apple
- Cinnamon – ½ teaspoon

- Sugar – ½ teaspoon

Instructions:
1. Place the biscuits on a cutting board and divide them in to half.
2. Take bowl and add cinnamon, apples and sugar.
3. Mix well and place them on the biscuit.
4. Cover the apple mixture with another biscuit slice.
5. Place them on the ninja foodi rack.
6. Choose air crisp function.
7. Close the air frying lid and set the temperature to 380F / 193C.
8. Cook for 5 minutes.
9. In another bowl add sugar powder and milk. Then mix them well.
10. Pour it over the fritters.
11. Serve and enjoy.

Nutritional information per serving: Calories: 317, Fat: 18g, Sodium: 356mg, Fiber: 1g, Sugar: 23g, Carbohydrate 59g, Protein 5g.

2. AIR FRIED PEACHES

Preparation Time: 5 Minutes

Cooking Time: 10 Minutes

Servings: 2

Ingredients:

- 2 Peaches
- Cubed butter – ¼ cup
- Whipped Cream
- Breadcrumbs – ¼ cup
- Sugar – ¼ cup

Instructions:

1. Slice the peaches and remove the seeds.
2. Place the peach slices on the ninja foodi basket.

3. Select air crisp mode.
4. Set the temperature at 350F / 177C.
5. Cook for 5 minutes.
6. Take a bowl and add bread crumbs, sugar and butter.
7. Mix them well.
8. Once the peaches are done taka them out and apply the bread crumb mixture over the peaches.
9. Then air fry for another 5 minutes at same temperature.
10. Take them out and let cool.
11. Apply whip cream and serve.

Nutritional information per serving: Calories: 46, Fat: 0.1g, Sodium: 0.5mg, Fiber: 2g, Sugar: 1.2g, Carbohydrate 12g, Protein 0.6g.

3. AIR FRIED SWEET PATTIES

Preparation Time: 15 Minutes

Cooking Time: 10 Minutes

Servings: 10

Ingredients:

- 10 Thawed patties wrappers
- 2 Apples
- Honey – 2 tbsp
- Vanilla extract - 1tsp
- Cinnamon – 1tsp
- Nutmeg – 1/8 tsp
- Corn flour – 2tsp
- Water – 1tsp
- 1 Egg
- Cooking oil

Instructions:

1. Set the ninja foodi in saute mode.
2. Add apples, nutmeg, cinnamon, vanilla, and honey.
3. Stir cook at "high" heat for 3 minutes.
4. Include the corn flour and water to the pot as well.
5. Then cook for 40 seconds.
6. Let it cool for some time.
7. Place the pattie wrappers on the cutting board and fill the filling to it.
8. Add 1 tbsp of apple mixture.

9. Roll the patties in half and use a fork to seal the edges.
10. Grease the ninja foodi basket with cooking spray.
11. Apply the beaten on the pattie by a cooking brush.
12. Place the patties in the basket. Do not over load it.
13. Select air crisp mode.
14. Close the air frying lid and set the temperature at 400F / 204C.
15. Cook for 10 minutes.
16. Cool and serve.

Nutritional information per serving: Calories: 164, Fat: 5g, Fiber: 3g, Carbohydrate 28g, Protein 3g.

4. BAKED APPLES

Preparation Time: 5 Minutes
Cooking Time: 12 Minutes
Servings: 2
Ingredients:

- 2 Apples
- Sugar – ¼ cup
- Butter – ¼ cup
- Ice cream
- Cracker crumbs – ¼ cup

Instructions:

1. Slice the apples.
2. Place the apple slices on the ninja foodi basket.
3. Select air crisp mode and set the temperature to 350F / 177C.
4. Cook for 6 minutes.
5. Take a bowl and add bread crumbs, sugar and butter.
6. Mix them well.
7. Once the apples are done taka them out and apply the bread crumb mixture over them.
8. Then air fry for another 6 minutes at same temperature.
9. Take them out and let cool.
10. Serve with ice cream.

Nutritional information per serving: Calories: 54, Fat: 1g, Fiber: 8g, Sugar: 3, Carbohydrate 15g, Protein 0.5g.

5. CHERRY PIE

Preparation Time: 5 Minutes

Cooking Time: 8 Minutes

Servings: 10

Ingredients:

- Pie crust - 1 pack
- Powdered sugar – 2 ¼ cups
- Milk – ¼ cup
- Chery filling - 1 can

Instructions:

1. Take the pie crusts out and place them on a cutting board.
2. Take one crust and fill with the filling.

3. Roll the pattie and seal the edges by applying water.
4. Place them in the basket of ninja foodi.
5. Choose air crisp function.
6. Set the temperature at 370F / 188C.
7. Cook for 8 minutes.
8. Take a bowl and add milk and sugar. Then mix well.
9. Once the patties are done pour the glaze over them and serve.

Nutritional information per serving: Calories: 450, Fat: 22g, Sodium: 365mg, Fiber: 1.5g, Sugar: 18g, Carbohydrate 61g, Protein 4g.

6. COCONUT CREAM CAKE

Preparation Time: 20 Minutes

Cooking Time: 50 Minutes

Servings: 8

Ingredients:

For the Cake

- 5 Eggs
- Sugar – 1 cup
- Flour – 1 cup
- Baking powder - 4 tsp
- Salt – ¼ tsp
- Milk – 1/3 cup
- Vanilla extract – 1 tbsp

For coconut sauce

- 1 Milk can – 14oz / 397g
- Milk – ¼ cup
- Whip cream – ¼ cup
- 1 Coconut milk can – 12oz / 340g

For the Vanilla Whipped Cream

- Whip cream – 2 cups
- Sugar powder – ¼ cup
- Vanilla extract – 2 tsp

Instructions:

1. Take the air fryer cake pan or the ninja foodi basket.
2. Place a parchment paper to the bottom of it.
3. Take mixing bowl and add eggs ¾ cup of sugar.
4. Then mix them well.
5. Now put ½ cup of milk, flour, vanilla, salt and baking powder (All the ingredients mentioned for the cake) mix well.
6. Put 1 ¼ cups of water to the ninja foodi cooking pot.
7. Now close the pressure cooker lid and set "high" pressure and cook for 50 minutes.
8. Once it is done use natural pressure release for 10 minutes. Then remove the remaining pressure from the pressure valve and open the lid.
9. Let the cake cool.
10. Take bowl and add all the ingredients mentioned in the coconut sauce.

11. Mix them well.
12. Pour the coconut sauce over the cake and keep in the fridge for 2 hours.
13. Take another bowl and add all ingredients mentioned in the vanilla whip cream.
14. Then keep it in the fridge as well.
15. Serve the cake with the whip cream.

Nutritional information per serving: Calories: 546, Fat: 18g, Sodium: 185mg, Fiber: 1.5g, Sugar: 75g, Carbohydrate 89g, Protein 11g.

7. COCOA MIXED STRAWBERRIES

Preparation Time: 15 Minutes

Cooking Time: 15 Minutes

Servings: 12

Ingredients:

- 12 Strawberries
- Cocoa powder – ½ cup
- Coconut oil – ½ cup
- Maple syrup – 1/3 cup
- Vanilla extract – ½ teaspoon

Instructions:
1. Add some 2 water cups in to the ninja foodi cooking pot and turn on the saute option.
2. Choose "medium" heat.
3. Take a blow and add coconut oil and other ingredients.
4. Mix them well.
5. Pour it to the cake pan and place in the ninja foodi rack.
6. Once the chocolate mixture gets smooth turn off the saute mode.
7. Take it out and let cool.
8. Serve with strawberries. Dip and enjoy.

Nutritional information per serving: Calories: 180, Fat: 7g, Sodium: 55mg, Fiber: 2g, Sugar: 18g, Carbohydrate 30g.

8. CHOCOLATE CUPCAKES

Preparation Time: 2 Minutes

Cooking Time: 12 Minutes

Servings: 6

Ingredients:

- 8 Chocolate pieces
- Milk Chocolate – 2oz / 60g
- Butter – 1 teaspoon
- Honey – 1 teaspoon
- Whip Cream – 1 teaspoon
- Self-rising flour – 1oz / 30g
- Cocoa powder – 0.5oz / 15g

Instructions:

1. For this you should have an air fryer baking pan (any size is ok).
2. Put the chocolate, honey and butter.
3. Select air crisp mode.
4. Cook for 3 minutes at 240F / 115C.
5. Put whip cream and mix well.
6. Take a bowl and add flour, cocoa powder, crushed milk chocolate and melted chocolate.
7. Well mix them.
8. Pour the cupcake to the cases and place in the ninja foodi basket.
9. Then cook further at 320F / 160C for 12 minutes.
10. Serve the cupcakes.

Nutritional information per serving: Calories: 97, Fat: 6g, Sodium: 10mg, Fiber: 2g, Sugar: 4g, Carbohydrate 14g, Protein 3g.

9. CEREAL FILLED BANANAS

Preparation Time: 10 Minutes
Cooking Time: 6 Minutes
Servings: 3
Ingredients:

- 3 Bananas
- Chocolate chips – 3 tbsp
- Marshmallows – 3 tbsp
- Cracker cereal – 3 tbsp
- Peanut butter chips – 3 tbsp

Instructions:

1. Make a cut lengthwise to the bananas.
2. Do the cut to make a pocket.
3. Put chocolate chips, peanut butter chips and marshmallows and cracker cereal in to the pocket.
4. Now move the bananas to the ninja foodi basket.
5. Choose air crisp mode.
6. Set the temperature to 400F / 204C and cook for 5 minutes.
7. When the peel gets black and banana is soft it is done.
8. Let them cool and serve.

Nutritional information per serving: Calories: 380, Fat: 12g, Sodium: 145mg, Fiber: 5g, Sugar: 15g, Carbohydrate 64g, Protein 8g.

10. CHOCOLATE LAVA CUBES

Preparation Time: 5 Minutes
Cooking Time: 12 Minutes
Servings: 6
Ingredients:

- Melted butter – ¼ cup
- Sugar – ½ cup
- 1 Egg
- Sugar free cocoa – 3 tablespoon
- Baking powder – 1/8 teaspoon
- Salt – 1/8 teaspoon
- Vanilla extract – ½ teaspoon
- Flour – 1/3 cup

Instructions:

1. Apply cooking spray in the ninja foodi basket and the baking pan.
2. Take a bowl and add vanilla and egg. Then mix well.
3. Put other ingredients and mix well.
4. Pour the mixture to the baking pan.
5. Place it in the ninja foodi.
6. Select air crisp mode.
7. Cook for 15 minutes at 325F / 163C.
8. Cool it and serve.

Nutritional information per serving: Calories: 129, Fat: 5g, Sodium: 50mg, Fiber: 0.5g, Sugar: 12g, Carbohydrate 22g, Protein 1.8g.

11. CHOCO MIXED ZUCCHINI BREAD

Preparation Time: 10 Minutes
Cooking Time: 18 Minutes
Servings: 8
Ingredients:

- Flour – ½ cup
- Cocoa powder – ¼ cup
- Chocolate chips – ½ cup
- Brown sugar – 6 tbsp
- Melted butter – 2 tbsp
- Olive oil – 2 tbsp
- Baking soda – ½ tsp
- Salt – ¼ tsp
- 1 Egg
- Vanilla extract – ½ tsp
- Shredded zucchini – ¾ cup

Instructions:

1. Take a bowl and put flour, cocoa powder, baking soda and salt. Then mix well and keep away.

2. In another bowl add brown sugar, egg, butter, vanilla and oil. Then mix them well.
3. Combine both mixtures and mix well.
4. Fold zucchinis and chocolate chips over it.
5. Move it to the baking pan and put in to the ninja foodi basket.
6. Choose air crisp mode.
7. Set the temperature as 310F / 154C and air fry for 35 minutes.
8. Cool and serve it.

Nutritional information per serving: Calories: 268, Fat: 8g, Sodium: 320mg, Fiber: 3.4g, Sugar: 2g, Carbohydrate 46g, Protein 5.6g.

12. DANISH CREAM CHEESE WITH RED CHERRIES

Preparation Time: 10 Minutes

Cooking Time: 5 Minutes

Servings: 5

Ingredients:

- Crescent rolls - 1 pack
- Sugar – 4 tbsp
- Cherry pie filling – ½ cup
- Vanilla – 1 tsp

Instructions:

1. Mix the crescent roll dough and divide it in to 5 parts.
2. Add the pie filling to each roll.

3. Place the rolls inside the ninja foodi basket.
4. Choose air crisp mode.
5. Set the temperature to 300F / 165C.
6. Cook for 5 minutes.
7. Take a bowl and mix milk and sugar.
8. Pour it over the cooked rolls and serve.

Nutritional information per serving: Calories: 153, Fat: 8g, Sodium: 14mg, Fiber: 0.3g, Sugar: 35g, Carbohydrate 38g, Protein 5g.

13. FRUITY DUMPLINGS

Preparation Time: 10 Minutes
Cooking Time: 10 Minutes
Servings: 8
Ingredients:

- Crescent rolls – 8oz / 227g
- 1 Sliced apple
- Butter – 4 tbsp
- Sugar – ½ cup
- Vanilla extract – ½ tsp
- Powdered cinnamon – 1 tsp
- Nutmeg powder – 1 pinch

Instructions:

1. Put the crescent roll dough and make it flat.

2. Put 1 apple slice and make one roll.
3. Turn on the ninja foodi and select the saute mode.
4. Add sugar, nutmeg, vanilla, cinnamon and butter to a bowl and mix well and stir until they become melted.
5. Pour the mixture over rolls.
6. Place the rolls in the rack and add some water to the cooking pot.
7. Close from the pressure cooking lid and cook for 10 minutes at "high" pressure.
8. Do a natural pressure release and serve with sprinkled sugar.

Nutritional information per serving: Calories: 267, Fat: 5g, Sodium: 265mg, Carbohydrate 41g, Protein 4g.

14. FRIED EGG ROLLS WITH CHOPPED APPLES

Preparation Time: 12 Minutes
Cooking Time: 8 Minutes
Servings: 6
Ingredients:

- Apple pie filling – 21oz / 595g
- Lime juice – ½ teaspoon
- 6 Egg roll wrappers
- Apple pie spice – ¼ teaspoon
- Powdered cinnamon – 1/8 teaspoon

- Flour – 1 tablespoon

Instructions:
1. Take a bowl add pie filling, lime juice, apple spice, cinnamon and flour.
2. Well mix them.
3. Take one egg roll wrapper and put one spoon of pie mixture to it.
4. Roll the wrapper.
5. Apply cooking spray over the wrapper and place in the ninja foodi basket.
6. Select air crisp mode and cook at 400F / 204C for 8 minutes.
7. Add sugar powder on top and serve.

Nutritional information per serving: Calories: 186, Fat: 14g, Sodium: 226mg, Fiber: 2.5g, Carbohydrate 45g, Protein 3g.

15. FRIED S'MORES

Preparation Time: 2 Minutes

Cooking Time: 6 Minutes

Servings: 5

Ingredients:

- 6 Graham crust
- Small marshmallows – 1 cup
- 12 Chocolate bars

Instructions:

1. Put 3 chocolate bars in to the graham crust.
2. Add marshmallows to it.
3. Choose air crisp function and cook at 370F / 187C for 7 minutes.

4. Take it out and serve.

Nutritional information per serving: Calories: 520, Fat: 28g, Sodium: 146mg, Fiber: 3g, Sugar: 48g, Carbohydrate 76g, Protein 8g.

16. FRENCH TOAST

Preparation Time: 5 Minutes

Cooking Time: 6 Minutes

Servings: 1

Ingredients:

- 4 Bread slices
- Vanilla – 1 tsp

- Cinnamon – ½ tsp
- 2 Eggs
- Milk – 2/3 cup

Instructions:

1. Take a bowl and put milk, eggs, cinnamon, and vanilla extract.
2. Well mix them.
3. Coat the bread sliced in the mixture.
4. Place them in the rack of the ninja foodi.
5. Select air crisp mode and set the temperature at 320F / 160C and cook for 5 minutes.
6. Take it out and serve.

Nutritional information per serving: Calories: 210, Fat: 8g, Sodium: 280mg, Fiber: 4g, Sugar: 7g, Carbohydrate 28g, Protein 6g.

17. FRIED APPLE FRIES

Preparation Time: 5 Minutes
Cooking Time: 8 Minutes
Servings: 3
Ingredients:

- 3 Apples
- Salt – 1 pinch
- ¾ Cinnamon powder – ¾ tsp

Instructions:
1. Slice the apples in to think pieces.
2. Turn on the ninja foodi and select air crisp mode then set the temperature to 390F / 198C.
3. Put the apple slices to the basket and air fry for 10 minutes.
4. Take them out sprinkle salt and cinnamon and serve.

Nutritional information per serving: Calories: 65, Sodium: 5mg, Fiber: 5g, Sugar: 12g, Carbohydrate 19g, Protein 5g.

18. HEALTHY BREAD PUDDING

Preparation Time: 10 Minutes

Cooking Time: 15 Minutes

Servings: 6

Ingredients:

- Bread (cut in to cubes) – 2 cups
- 1 Egg
- Vanilla– ½ teaspoon
- Sugar – ¼ cup
- Heavy cream – 2/3 cup

Instructions:

1. Take the baking pan and apply some cooking oil over it.
2. Now place the bread pieces to the pan.
3. Take a bowl and put whip cream, egg, sugar and vanilla.
4. Now pour the mixture over bread.
5. Place the baking pan on the rack of the ninja foodi.
6. Choose air crisp mode and set the temperature to 350F / 176C and cook for 15 minutes.
7. Take it out check for the desired thickness and serve.

Nutritional information per serving: Calories: 375, Fat: 14g, Sodium: 426mg, Fiber: 4g, Sugar: 15g, Carbohydrate 53g, Protein 14g.

19. LOW CARB CHEESE CAKE

Preparation Time: 10 Minutes

Cooking Time: 1 Hour 50 Minutes

Servings: 7

Ingredients:

For crust,

- Olive oil spray
- Melted butter – 3 tablespoons
- Salt – 1 pinch
- Crackers (crushed) – 1 cup

For cheesecake,

- Cream cheese – 15oz / 425g
- Powdered sugar – ½ cup

- Brown sugar – ¼ cup
- Sour cream – ¼ cup
- Salt – ¼ teaspoon
- 2 Eggs
- Flour – 1 tablespoon
- Vanilla extract – 1 teaspoon
- Whip cream

Instructions:

1. Take a bowl and put cracker crumbs, butter and salt. Then mix well.
2. Take an oiled baking pan (air fryer type) sprinkle the mixture over it and keep in the fridge for 20 minutes.
3. In another bowl put cream cheese, sugar, sour cream, butter, flour, vanilla and eggs.
4. Then mix everything well from a mixer.
5. Take the refrigerated pan and pour the mixture over it.
6. Put some water in to the ninja foodi cooking pot.
7. Cover the pan with an aluminum foil and place on the rack.
8. Put the pressure cooking lid and pressure cook for 35 minutes at "high" pressure.
9. Go for a natural pressure release.
10. Now take the cheese cake and place in the fridge for 1h and 30 minutes and serve.

Nutritional information per serving: Calories: 467, Fat: 30g, Sodium: 305mg, Fiber: 1g, Sugar: 14g, Carbohydrate 23g, Protein 7.5g.

20. LOW SUGAR CHOCOLATE CAKE

Preparation Time: 5 Minutes
Cooking Time: 10 Minutes
Servings: 6
Ingredients:
- Whole wheat flour – ½ cup
- Almond Milk – 1/3 cup
- 2 Eggs
- Powdered sugar – ½ cups

- Vanilla – 1 teaspoon
- Cocoa powder – 1/3 cup
- Baking powder – 1 teaspoon
- Salt – ¼ teaspoon

Instructions:

1. Take bowl and put all the ingredients and mix well.
2. Take air fryer size baking pan and apply oil on it.
3. Pour the mixture to the baking pan.
4. Choose air crisp mode.
5. Set the temperature at 350F / 176C in the ninja foodi and set the time for 10 minutes.
6. Once it is done enjoy.

Nutritional information per serving: Calories: 207, Fat: 17g, Sodium: 59mg, Fiber: 4.6g, Carbohydrate 3.5g, Protein 8g.

21. LOW SUGAR BROWNIES

Preparation Time: 10 Minutes

Cooking Time: 1 Hour

Servings: 8

Ingredients:

- Cooking oil spray
- Melted butter – ¾ cup
- Cocoa powder – ½ cup
- 4 Eggs
- Vanilla – 1 teaspoon
- Flour – ¾ cup
- Salt - ½ teaspoon
- Chocolate chips – 1 cup
- Water – 1 cup

- Powdered sugar – 1½ cup

Instructions:
1. Take the baking pan for this recipes as well.
2. Apply the cooking spray on it.
3. Take a bowl and put butter, cocoa powder and sugar. Then mix well.
4. Include eggs and vanilla as well.
5. Pour the mixture to the baking pan and sprinkle chocolate chips.
6. Cover the pan with an aluminum foil paper.
7. Put water in to the cooking pot. Then place the pan on the rack and close the pressure cooking lid.
8. Set in to "high" pressure and cook for 35 minutes.
9. Once the pressure cooking is done perform a quick pressure release (Check chapter 3 for more info).
10. Let it cool for 10 minutes and serve.

Nutritional information per serving: Calories: 113, Fat: 7g, Sodium: 83mg, Sugar: 12g, Carbohydrate 15g, Protein 2g.

22. LEMON FLAVORED CHEESE CAKE

Preparation Time: 25 Minutes

Cooking Time: 1 Hour 25 Minutes

Servings: 8

Ingredients:
- Cracker crumbs – 1 cup
- Melted butter – 3 tbsp
- Sugar – 1 tbsp
- Lemon zest – 1 tbsp
- Whipping cream – ½ cup
- Sugar powder – 2tbsp
- Vanilla – ½ tsp
- Cream cheese – 8oz / 227g
- Milk – 1 can

- Lemon juice – 1/3 cup
- 1 Egg

Instructions:

1. Take a bowl and put cracker crumbs, butter, and sugar.
2. Crush the crumbs and mix well. Then keep in the fridge for 10 minutes.
3. In another bowl add cream cheese and mix them well.
4. Add milk to it as well.
5. Include lemon juice egg and lemon zest.
6. Now put the mixture in to the frozen crust.
7. Pour 1 water cup to the ninja foodi cooking pot.
8. Place the baking pan in rack and close with the pressure cooking lid.
9. Cook for 25 minutes at "high" pressure.
10. Once it is completed do a quick pressure release (as mentioned in chapter 3)
11. Take it out and let it cool.
12. Then put it back in the fridge for 1 hour.
13. Then take it out and serve.

Nutritional information per serving: Calories: 478, Fat: 28g, Sodium: 274mg, Fiber: 1g, Sugar: 45g, Carbohydrate 53g, Protein 10g.

23. LOW CARB CHOCOLATE DONUTS

Preparation Time: 15 Minutes

Cooking Time: 15 Minutes

Servings: 15

Ingredients:

- Whole wheat flour – 1cup
- Baking soda – ½ teaspoon
- Chopped chocolate – 1oz / 28g
- 1 Egg
- Yogurt – ¼ cup
- Brown sugar – 3 tablespoon
- Cocoa powder – 3 tablespoon
- Butter - 1½ tablespoon

Instructions:

1. Take a bowl add flour, baking powder and baking powder, cocoa powder and sugar.
2. Heat up the butter and chocolate and melt them.
3. Now add egg and yogurt to the bowl mentioned earlier.
4. Include the melted chocolate butter mix the bowl.
5. Keep the bowl in the fridge for 30 minutes.
6. Then take the bowl out from the fridge.
7. Take a scoop of the mixture and make balls from hand.
8. Apply some cooking spray over the basket of the ninja foodi.
9. Select air crisp function and set the temperature to 350F / 176C.
10. Cook for 12 minutes and serve.

Nutritional information per serving: Calories: 23, Fat: 2g, Sodium: 39mg, Fiber: 1g, Sugar: 2g, Carbohydrate 3g, Protein 1g.

24. MIXED FOOD CAKE

Preparation Time: 10 Minutes
Cooking Time: 20 Minutes
Servings: 4
Ingredients:

- 2 Eggs
- Sugar – 2 tablespoons
- Vanilla – ¼ teaspoon
- Whip cream – 8oz / 227g
- Strawberries sliced – 1 cup
- Flour – ¼ cup
- Baking soda – ¼ teaspoon

Instructions:

1. Take a bowl and add sugar and eggs.
2. Mix them well.
3. Include vanilla, flour, baking soda and mix further.
4. Apply oil on the air fryer baking pan and move the mixture to it.
5. Choose air crisp ,ode and set the temperature to 325F / 163C and cook for 15 minutes.
6. Create another layer like this by following these same steps.
7. Put one layer and add the whip cream over it.
8. Then put the second layer over it.
9. Now refrigerate them again for 30 minutes.

10. Take it out and serve with strawberries.

Nutritional information per serving: Calories: 105, Fat: 4g, Sodium: 28mg, Fiber: 1g, Sugar: 2g, Carbohydrate 15g, Protein 3g.

25. OATS WITH CHOPPED APPLES

Preparation Time: 5 Minutes

Cooking Time: 25 Minutes

Servings: 2

Ingredients:

- 2 Apples (chopped)
- Lime juice - 1 tsp

- Brown sugar – 2 tbsp
- Flour - 2 ½ tbsp
- Sugar – 2 tbsp
- Salt – 1 pinch
- 1 Sliced banana
- Berries – ½ cup
- Oats - 3 tbsp
- Butter – 2 tbsp

Instructions:

1. Cut the apple in to small pieces to a bowl.
2. Add lime juice and sugar.
3. Mix them well.
4. Cover with an aluminum paper and choose air crisp function.
5. Then cook for 15 minutes at 350F / 177C.
6. Take another bowl and put oats, flour, sugar, salt, butter and mix well.
7. Mix the apple with the mixture.
8. Air fry for another 5 minutes at same temperature.
9. Put the banana slices and berries serve.

Nutritional information per serving: Calories: 355, Fat: 14g, Fiber: 7g, Sugar: 38g, Carbohydrate 62g, Protein 3g

26. PUMPKIN PIE

Preparation Time: 5 Minutes

Cooking Time: 8 Minutes

Servings: 8

Ingredients:

- Crescent rolls – 1 can
- Pumpkin puree - ½ cup
- Salt – 1/8 tsp
- Melted butter – 3 tbsp
- Pumpkin pie spice – 2 tsp

Instructions:

1. Put crescent rolls on a cutting board and roll out them.
2. Take a mixing bowl and add pumpkin puree pie spice and salt and mix them well.
3. Put the mixture on crescent roll and roll them.
4. Place in the ninja foodi basket and do not over crowd.
5. Apply melted butter on the rolls put.
6. Select air crisp mode.
7. Cook for 5 minutes at 325F / 163C.
8. Take them out and enjoy.

Nutritional information per serving: Calories: 218, Fat: 13g, Sodium: 107mg, Fiber: 1g, Sugar: 15g, Carbohydrate 24g, Protein 2g.

27. REFRESHING BANANA CAKE

Preparation Time: 10 Minutes

Cooking Time: 50 Minutes

Servings: 2

Ingredients:

- Olive oil spray
- Water – 1 cup
- Chocolate chips– 1cup
- Caramel– ¾ cup
- 2 Bananas
- Brown sugar – 2/3 cup
- 2 Eggs

- Melted butter – 4 tablespoons
- Vanilla – 1 teaspoon
- Flour – 1 ¼ cups
- Baking soda – 1 teaspoon
- Salt – ½ teaspoon
- Coconut– 1 cup

Instructions:

1. Take the air fryer baking pan and apply olive oil spray.
2. Put water to the ninja foodi cooking pot.
3. Take a bowl and mash banana and add sugar, eggs, melted butter and vanilla.
4. Then mix them well.
5. Combine flour, baking soda and salt as well.
6. After that put coconut, chocolate chips and caramel to the mixture.
7. Pour the mixture to the baking pan and cover with an aluminum paper.
8. Place in the rack and close with the pressure cooking lid and cook for 50 minutes at "high" pressure.
9. Do 15 minute natural release once cooking is done. (Refer chapter 3 for more).
10. Keep it in the refrigerator and serve.
11. Then serve the cake.

Nutritional information per serving: Calories: 247, Fat: 8g, Sodium: 232mg, Fiber: 1.8g, Sugar: 18g, Carbohydrate 40g, Protein 4g.

28. SLICED BANANA WITH PEANUT BUTTER

Preparation Time: 15 Minutes

Cooking Time: 5 Minutes

Servings: 12

Ingredients:

- 1 Sliced banana
- 12 Wrappers
- Peanut butter – ½ cup
- Coconut oil – 2 tsp

Instructions:

1. Put banana slices to a bowl.
2. Then place one banana slice and peanut butter in to the middle of each wrapper and rollit.
3. Move it to the ninja foodi basket.
4. Select air crisp mode and cook at 380F / 193C for 5 minutes and enjoy.

Nutritional information per serving: Calories: 440, Fat: 20g, Sodium: 1300mg, Carbohydrate 42g, Protein 10g.

29. SWEET BERRY TARTS

Preparation Time: 15 Minutes

Cooking Time: 10 Minutes

Servings: 5

Ingredients:

- 2 Pie crusts
- Corn flour – 1 tsp
- Yogurt – ½ cup
- Low fat cream cheese – 1oz / 28g
- Sugar – 1 tsp
- Strawberry – 1/3 cup
- Coconut oil

Instructions:

1. Place the pie crust on the cutting board.
2. Cut 5 rectangles from the pie crust.
3. Put corn flour and other ingredients to a bowl and mix well.
4. Place them in to the pie crust as well.
5. Apply some oil over the crust and place in the ninja foodi basket.
6. Select air crisp function.
7. Then cook at 370F / 188C for 10 minutes.
8. Take another bowl and mix cream cheese, yogurt and sugar.

9. When the tarts are done take out and apply the cream cheese mixture on the top and serve.

Nutritional information per serving: Calories: 274, Fat: 14g, Carbohydrate 34g, Protein 5g.

30. SLICED BANANA WITH MIXED NUTS

Preparation Time: 5 Minutes
Cooking Time: 10 Minutes
Servings: 2
Ingredients:

- 1 Sliced banana
- Brown sugar – ½ teaspoon

- Chopped nuts (toasted) – 1 tablespoon
- Cinnamon – ¼ teaspoon

Instructions:

1. Take bowl and put cinnamon and sugar.
2. Mix them and set aside.
3. Then grease the air fryer baking pan with oil.
4. Put banana slices to the pan and sprinkle the sugar and cinnamon mix over it.
5. Select air crisp function.
6. Set the temperature at 400F / 204C and cook for 5 minutes.
7. Serve with chopped nuts.

Nutritional information per serving: Calories: 114, Fat: 4g, Sodium: 3mg, Fiber: 2g, Sugar: 8g, Carbohydrate 18g, Protein 2g.

CHAPTER 11
VEGETARIAN RECIPES

1. AIR FRIED CORN

Preparation Time: 5 Minutes
Cooking Time: 20 Minutes
Servings: 4
Ingredients:

- Corn – 4 ears
- Olive oil – 2 tbsp
- Salt – 1 tsp
- Powdered pepper – 1 tsp

Instructions:

1. First turn the ninja foodi on and select the air crisp mode and pre heat to 400F / 204C.
2. Apply olive oil over corns.
3. Add salt and pepper over it.
4. Place the corn in the olive oil applied ninja foodi basket.
5. Close the air fryer lid and cook for 20 minutes.
6. Turn the corns after 10 minutes.
7. Put some parsley over top and serve.

Nutritional information per serving: Calories: 58, Fat: 1.5g, Sodium: 153mg, Fiber: 5g, Carbohydrate: 10g, Protein: 1g.

2. AIR FRIED SPICY TOFU

Preparation Time: 30 Minutes

Cooking Time: 15 Minutes

Servings: 2

Ingredients:

- Tofu – 15oz / 425g
- Onion powder – 1 tsp
- Salt – ¼ tsp
- Sesame oil – 2 tbsp
- Garlic powder – 1 tsp

Instructions:

1. Make tofu in to small pieces. And squeeze out much liquid as possible.
2. Then put the tofu pieces in to a bowl and add onion powder, sesame oil salt and powdered garlic.
3. Mix well and keep a side for 15 minutes.
4. Place the tofu in your ninja foodi basket.
5. Do not over crowd it.
6. Select air crisp mode and cook at 375F / 190C for 15 minutes.
7. Let them cool and serve.

Nutritional information per serving: Calories: 36, Fat: 2.7g, Sodium: 2mg, Fiber: 0.5g, Sugar: 0.3g, Carbohydrate: 2g, Protein: 3g.

3. BAKED LINED POTATOES

Preparation Time: 15 Minutes

Cooking Time: 40 Minutes

Servings: 4

Ingredients:

- Potatoes – 2lb / 907g
- Chopped parsley – ¼ cup
- Salt – 1 tsp
- Olive oil – 4 tbsp
- Minced garlic – 1 tbsp

Instructions:

1. Take potatoes and wash the skin well.
2. Then cut them in to slices from the top. Don't entirely cut the slice. (It should remain as a one potato from the bottom).
3. Apply olive oil over the potatoes.
4. Select air crisp mode and cook the potatoes at 410F / 210C for 30 minutes.
5. Make sure every side is getting equally fried.
6. Till its done take a bowl and put parsley, garlic, salt and olive oil.
7. Mix well and sprinkle over the potatoes when they are done and serve.

Nutritional information per serving: Calories: 112, Fat: 12g, Sodium: 63mg, Fiber: 3g, Sugar: 1g, Carbohydrate: 25g, Protein: 3g.

4. BATTERED CUCUMBER FRIES

Preparation Time: 10 Minutes
Cooking Time: 15 Minutes
Servings: 4
Ingredients:

- 2 Sliced cucumbers
- Breadcrumbs – ¾ cup
- Garlic powder – ½ teaspoon
- 1 Egg
- Olive oil spray
- Salt – ½ teaspoon

Instructions:

1. Put the egg in to a bowl.
2. Add breadcrumbs to another plate.
3. Mix salt and garlic powder with breadcrumbs.
4. Now dip the cucumber slices in egg and then breadcrumb mixture.
5. Place them in the ninja foodi basket.
6. Choose air crisp function and set the temperature at 350F / 177C and cook for 10 minutes.
7. Take them out and serve.

Nutritional information per serving: Calories: 70, Fat: 2g, Sodium: 684mg, Fiber: 1g, Sugar: 2g, Carbohydrate: 11g, Protein: 4g.

5. CRUNCHY SLICED POTATOES

Preparation Time: 15 Minutes

Cooking Time: 15 Minutes

Servings: 6

Ingredients:

- 4 Sliced potatoes
- Olive oil – 4 tablespoons
- Pepper – ½ teaspoon
- Garlic powder – 1 teaspoon
- Salt – 1 teaspoon

Instructions:

1. Take a bowl and add potatoes and ingredients.
2. Then mix well.
3. Choose air crisp mode.
4. Move it to the basket and cook for 15 minutes at 380F / 193C.
5. Cool and serve when they are done.

Nutritional information per serving: Calories: 245, Fat: 12g, Sodium: 493mg, Fiber: 5g, Sugar: 1g, Carbohydrate: 30g, Protein: 8g.

6. CARROT FRIES

Preparation Time: 5 Minutes
Cooking Time: 15 Minutes
Servings: 4
Ingredients:

- Carrots cut in the cubes – 1lb / 454g
- Olive oil – 1 tbsp
- Cumin – ¼ tsp
- Salt as required

Instructions:

1. Mix carrots, olive oil, cumin and salt in a bowl.
2. Choose air crisp function.

3. Put in to the basket and cook at 370F / 187C for 15 minutes and serve.

Nutritional information per serving: Calories: 78, Fat: 4g, Sodium: 80mg, Fiber: 3g, Sugar: 5g, Carbohydrate: 12g, Protein: 1g.

7. CHEESY BEAN FRIES

Preparation Time: 10 Minutes
Cooking Time: 20 Minutes
Servings: 2
Ingredients:
- Beans – ½ lb / 227g
- Diced garlic – 1 clove
- Shredded parmesan – 2 tablespoon
- Olive Oil – 1 tablespoon
- Ketchup

Instructions:
1. Cut the beans in to small pieces.
2. Mix with garlic, cheese and olive oil.
3. Select air crisp mode.
4. Put in to the basket and cook at 350F / 177C for 20 minutes.
5. Serve with some ketchup.

Nutritional information per serving: Calories: 120, Fat: 8g, Carbohydrate: 12g, Protein: 3g.

8. CRISPY SPROUTS

Preparation Time: 5 Minutes
Cooking Time: 10 Minutes
Servings: 1
Ingredients:
- Brussels sprouts– 1 lb / 454g
- Olive oil spray
- Salt – ¼ teaspoon
- Garlic powder – ¼ teaspoon

Instructions:

1. Take brussels sprouts and cut in half.
2. Take a bowl and add garlic powder, salt and sprouts.
3. Then spray some olive oil over them and cook for 5 minutes at 365F / 185C under air crisp mode.
4. Serve when they are done.

Nutritional information per serving: Calories: 46, Sodium: 68mg, Fiber: 5g, Carbohydrate: 10g, Protein: 3g.

9. CABBAGE WEDGES

Preparation Time: 5 Minutes
Cooking Time: 8 Minutes
Servings: 8
Ingredients:

- 1 Cabbage
- Olive oil – 1 tablespoon
- Onion powder – 1/8 teaspoon
- Garlic salt – 1/8 teaspoon
- Old bay – ¼ teaspoon

Instructions:

1. Cut the cabbage in to small slices.
2. Take a bowl and add the ingredients and mix well.
3. Place the cabbage slices in the basket and select air crisp, then cook for 5 minutes at 350F / 177C.

4. Take them out and serve.

Nutritional information per serving: Calories: 45, Fat: 2g, Sodium: 56mg, Fiber: 3g, Sugar: 5g, Carbohydrate: 7g, Protein: 1g.

10. CRISPY CAULI FLOWERS

Preparation Time: Minutes

Cooking Time: Minutes

Servings:

Ingredients:

- Cauliflower – ½ lb / 277g
- Minced garlic – 1 clove
- Salt & pepper
- Olive oil – 1 tbsp
- Shredded parmesan cheese– 1 tbsp

Instructions:

1. Take a bowl and add cauliflower and other ingredients.
2. Place them in the ninja foodi basket and sprinkle some cheese over them.
3. Choose air crisp mode and cook for 10 minutes at 390F / 198C.
4. Serve warm.

Nutritional information per serving: Calories: 112, Fat: 8g, Sodium: 76mg, Fiber: 3g, Sugar: 1g, Carbohydrate: 7g, Protein: 4g.

11. CUCUMBER PASTA MIX

Preparation Time: 10 Minutes
Cooking Time: 10 Minutes
Servings: 4
Ingredients:

- Olive oil spray
- Minced garlic – 3 cloves
- Water - 1 cup
- Sliced cucumber – 4 cups
- Chopped spinach – 2 cups
- Feta cheese – 1 ¼ cup
- 1 Egg
- Parmesan cheese – 1 tbsp

- Pasta – 1½ cup
- Mozzarella cheese – 1 cup
- Pepper powder
- Basil
- Tomato sauce – 1 cup

Instructions:
1. Put pasta and water to the cooking pot.
2. Then pressure cook for 5 minutes at high pressure.
3. Do a quick pressure release.
4. Open the lid and add cucumber, pepper, tomato sauce, spinach, basil, mozzarella cheese and egg.
5. Mix everything well.
6. Select saute mode and cook for 10 minutes at high heat.
7. When the desired thickness comes turn off the function and serve to the table.

Nutritional information per serving: Calories: 267, Fat: 17g, Sodium: 815mg, Fiber: 3g, Sugar: 4g, Carbohydrate: 10g, Protein: 20g.

12. EASY VEGETABLE SOUP

Preparation Time: 10 Minutes

Cooking Time: 45 Minutes

Servings: 6

Ingredients:

- Chopped cabbage – 2 cups
- Cauliflower – 2 cups
- 2 Sliced carrots
- Sliced celery – 2 stalks
- 1 Chopped red bell pepper
- Chopped cucumber
- Olive oil – 1 tablespoon

- 1 Diced onion
- Minced garlic – 4 cloves
- Salt
- Pepper powder
- Chopped tomato – 1 tablespoon
- Beans – 1can
- Diced tomatoes – 1 can
- Vegetable broth – 4 cups
- Pepper - ¾ teaspoon
- Chopped parsley

Instructions:

1. Select saute mode for this as well.
2. Add onion, oil, garlic salt and pepper.
3. Stir cook till onions get tender.
4. Include other ingredients.
5. Include the tomato and cook further for 1 minute. Stop the saute mode.
6. Close the pressure cooking lid and cook for 12 minutes at high pressure.
7. Do a quick pressure release.
8. Open the lid and serve with salt and pepper.

Nutritional information per serving: Calories: 156, Fat: 2g, Sodium: 925mg, Fiber: 5g, Sugar: 10g, Carbohydrate: 29g, Protein: 5g.

13. FRIED EGGPLANT SLICES

Preparation Time: 15 Minutes

Cooking Time: 12 Minutes

Servings: 6

Ingredients:

- 1 Sliced eggplant
- Flour – ½ cup
- Pepper – ¼ teaspoon
- Salt – 1/8 teaspoon
- Cooking spray
- 1 Egg
- Panko– 2 cups
- Seasoning powder – 1½ tablespoons

Instructions:

1. Put egg to one bowl.
2. Take another bowl and put panko & flour.
3. Then put the seasoning to the other bowl.
4. Dip each eggplant slice in flout mix.
5. Then egg mix and finally in the seasoning.
6. Place them in the ninja foodi basket and set the temperature to 380F / 193C under air crisp mode.
7. Air fry for 8 minutes.
8. Take them out and serve when they become cool.

Nutritional information per serving: Calories: 150, Fat: 2g, Sodium: 206mg, Fiber: 4g, Sugar: 5g, Carbohydrate: 28g, Protein: 5g.

14. FRIED SLICED BEETS

Preparation Time: 10 Minutes

Cooking Time: 12 Minutes

Servings: 4

Ingredients:

- 2 Peeled beets
- Pepper – ¼ teaspoon
- Salt – ¼ teaspoon
- Olive oil – 2 tablespoons

Instructions:

1. Cut the beets in to cubes.
2. Add them to a bowl and add olive oil, salt and pepper.
3. Mix well and move to the ninja foodi basket.

4. Select air crisp function.
5. Set the temperature to 370F / 188C and cook for 12 minutes.
6. Enjoy the dish.

Nutritional information per serving: Calories: 81, Fat: 7g, Sodium: 324mg, Fiber: 1g, Sugar: 3g, Carbohydrate: 5g, Protein: 1g.

15. FRIED KALE CHIPS

Preparation Time: 5 Minutes

Cooking Time: 5 Minutes

Servings: 2

Ingredients:

- Kale – 1 bunch
- Olive oil – 1 tbsp
- Salt – ½ tsp

Instructions:

1. Take a bowl and mix all the ingredients together.
2. Put them in to ninja foodi basket.
3. Then choose air crisp mode and then set the temperature to 390F / 198C and cook for 5 minutes.

4. Then serve in a dish.

Nutritional information per serving: Calories: 189, Fat: 10g, Sodium: 268mg, Fiber: 3g, Sugar: 1g, Carbohydrate: 23g, Protein: 8g.

16. FRIED ZUCCHINI SLICES

Preparation Time: 10 Minutes
Cooking Time: 12 Minutes
Servings: 5
Ingredients:

- 2 Sliced zucchinis
- Breadcrumbs – ¾ cup
- Garlic powder – ½ teaspoon
- 1 Egg (whisked)
- Cooking spray
- Salt – ½ teaspoon

Instructions:

1. Take a bowl and put egg to it.
2. In another bowl for breadcrumbs.
3. Take zucchini slices and dip them in the egg and breadcrumbs.
4. Apply cooking spray over zucchini slices as well as the basket.

5. Move the zucchini to the basket and select air crisp mode, then set the temperature at 350F / 177C and select air fry mode and cook for 15 minutes.
6. Flip other side after 7 minutes.
7. Serve them once they get heat reduced.

Nutritional information per serving: Calories: 43, Fat: 1g, Sodium: 452mg, Fiber: 1g, Sugar: 0.8g, Carbohydrate: 6g, Protein: 2g.

17. FRIED VEGGIES WITH BALANCED NUTRITIONS

Preparation Time: 10 Minutes

Cooking Time: 10 Minutes

Servings: 5

Ingredients:

- 2 Sliced zucchinis
- 1 Small sliced pumpkin
- Seasoning – ¾ teaspoon
- Garlic powder – ½ teaspoon
- Salt – ¼ teaspoon
- 5 Sliced Mushrooms
- Olive oil – ½ cup

- ½ a sliced onion

Instructions:
1. Add pumpkin, mushroom, onion and zucchini to a bowl.
2. Put olive oil, seasoning, garlic powder and salt.
3. Then mix well.
4. Choose air crisp mode.
5. Set the temperature to 400F / 204C and cook for 10 minutes.
6. Serve the dish.

Nutritional information per serving: Calories: 184, Fat: 18g, Sodium: 203mg, Fiber: 2g, Sugar: 1g, Carbohydrate: 5g, Protein: 2g.

18. FRIED SLICED PUMPKIN

Preparation Time: 5 Minutes
Cooking Time: 30 Minutes
Servings: 4
Ingredients:
- 1 Small pumpkin
- Cinnamon – ½ tsp
- Salt
- Pepper powder
- Olive oil – 1 tbsp

Instructions:

1. Slice the pumpkin in to small chunks.
2. Remove the seeds.
3. Add them to a bowl and mix with olive oil, salt, pepper and cinnamon.
4. Move them to the basket.
5. Select air crisp mode.
6. Cook in your ninja foodi at 350F / 177C for 30 minutes.
7. Take them out and serve.

Nutritional information per serving: Calories: 128, Fat: 4g, Sodium: 8mg, Fiber: 4g, Sugar: 6g, Carbohydrate: 25g, Protein: 3g.

19. HEALTHY ASPARAGUS BITES

Preparation Time: 2 Minutes
Cooking Time: 10 Minutes
Servings: 4
Ingredients:

- Asparagus - 1 bunch
- Olive oil spray
- Garlic salt

Instructions:

1. Remove the stems of the asparagus.
2. Move them to the ninja foodi basket.

3. Spray some oil and sprinkle garlic salt over them.
4. Choose air crisp mode and cook at 400F / 204C for 4 minutes.
5. Serve the dish.

Nutritional information per serving: Calories: 105, Fat: 2g, Sodium: 208mg, Fiber: 1g, Carbohydrate: 8g, Protein: 7g.

20. PICKLE FRIES

Preparation Time: 15 Minutes
Cooking Time: 35 Minutes
Servings: 6
Ingredients:

- 12 Pickle slices
- Hot sauce– ¼ tsp
- Panko – 1 ½ cups
- Onion powder – ½ tsp
- Dried dill – ½ tsp
- Flour – ½ cup
- 2 Eggs
- Water – 1 tbsp
- Cooking spray

Instructions:

1. First dry the pickles from a paper towel.
2. Add some flour to a bowl.

3. Put eggs, water and hot sauce to another bowl.
4. In a spate bowl add panko and spices.
5. Make sure each pickle slice is going through flour, eggs and panko bowls.
6. Then place in the ninja foodi basket.
7. Put some cooking spray over the pickles.
8. Select air crisp mode and set the temperature at 400F /204C and cook for 5 minutes.
9. Cool for 3 minutes.
10. Then serve.

Nutritional information per serving: Calories: 57, Fat: 1g, Sodium: 70mg, Fiber: 1g, Sugar: 1g, Carbohydrate: 8g, Protein: 2g.

21. POTATO BEAN TWISTER

Preparation Time: 10 Minutes
Cooking Time: 30 Minutes
Servings: 5
Ingredients:

- Beans (trimmed) – 12oz / 340g
- Garlic salt – ½ teaspoon
- Olive oil spray
- Sliced potatoes – 2lb / 907g

Instructions:

1. Put the potatoes and beans to the ninja foodi basket.
2. Make sure you add some olive oil to the basket before loading vegetables.
3. Then add the garlic salt over the veggies.
4. Choose air crisp function and cook at 380F / 193C for 30 minutes.
5. Enjoy after cool them.

Nutritional information per serving: Calories: 134, Fat: 4g, Sodium: 223mg, Fiber: 3g, Sugar: 3g, Carbohydrate: 21g, Protein: 4g.

22. PANKO COATED OKRA

Preparation Time: 15 Minutes
Cooking Time: 10 Minutes
Servings: 6
Ingredients:

- Okra (cut in to cubes) - ½ lb / 227g
- Pepper – ¼ teaspoon
- 1 Egg
- Breadcrumbs – 1 cup
- Salt – 1 teaspoon

Instructions:

1. Take a bowl and out egg, salt, breadcrumbs and pepper.
2. Put the okra cubes in to the egg mix and cost well.
3. Select air crisp mode of your ninja foodi ad set the temperature to 355F / 179C.
4. Cook for 10 minutes.
5. Let them cool for 2 minutes and serve.

Nutritional information per serving: Calories: 64, Fat: 1g, Sodium: 475mg, Fiber: 2g, Sugar: 1g, Carbohydrate: 10g, Protein: 3g.

23. ROASTED THIN POTATOES

Preparation Time: 10 Minutes
Cooking Time: 45 Minutes
Servings: 4
Ingredients:

- 4 Sliced potatoes
- Salt – 2 tablespoons
- Olive oil – 3 tablespoons

Instructions:

1. Clean the potatoes with water and dry them.
2. Then apply salt over the potatoes.
3. Apply some olive oil over them as well.

4. Now put them inside the ninja foodi basket.
5. Close the air fryer lid and select air crisp mode.
6. Then set the temperature to 400F / 204C and cook for 30 minutes.
7. Then take them out and serve.

Nutritional information per serving: Calories: 185, Fat: 7g, Sodium: 3500mg, Fiber: 5g, Carbohydrate: 25g, Protein: 5g.

24. STEAMED CHOY SALAD

Preparation Time: 10 Minutes

Cooking Time: 4 Minutes

Servings: 4

Ingredients:

- 1 Bok choy
- Water – ¼ cup
- Rice wine – 1 tablespoon
- Minced garlic – 1 tablespoon
- Soy sauce – ¼ cup

Instructions:

1. Remove the ends of bok choy.

2. Put bok choy and other ingredients to the ninja foodi cooking pot.
3. Close the pressure cooking lid and cook for 4 minutes at high pressure.
4. This time do a quick pressure release (refer chapter 3).
5. Open the lid and serve.

Nutritional information per serving: Calories: 37, Fat: 1g, Sodium: 945mg, Fiber: 2g, Sugar: 3g, Carbohydrate: 6g, Protein: 5g.

25. SPICY SWEET POTATOES

Preparation Time: 10 Minutes

Cooking Time: 20 Minutes

Servings: 4

Ingredients:

- Sliced sweet potatoes – 1lb / 454g
- Parmesan cheese - 2 tablespoons
- Olive oil - 2 tablespoons
- Powdered black pepper – 1 teaspoon
- Salt – 1 teaspoon
- Red pepper flakes – ½ teaspoon
- Chopped parsley - 1 tablespoon

Instructions:

1. Take a bowl and add potatoes and olive oil.
2. Then mix well.
3. After that add parmesan and salt.
4. Further mix them.
5. Grease the ninja foodi basket with olive oil.
6. Select air crisp mode and set temperature to 400F / 204C and cook for 10 minutes.
7. Take them out sprinkle some parsley and serve.

Nutritional information per serving: Calories: 176, Fat: 5g, Sodium: 380mg, Fiber: 7g, Sugar: 8g, Carbohydrate: 45g, Protein: 5g.

26. SPINACH POTATO TWIST

Preparation Time: 5 Minutes
Cooking Time: 40 Minutes
Servings: 5
Ingredients:

- 4 Potatoes
- Salt & pepper
- Sour cream
- Vegetable oil – 2 tablespoons
- Spinach – 1 bunch

Instructions:

1. Cut the potatoes in to bite sized pieces.
2. Put them to a bowl and salt and pepper.
3. Then mix well.
4. Put the mixture to the oiled basket.
5. Put the spinach leaves on the top of potato slices.
6. Select air crisp mode and set the temperature to 390F / 198C.
7. Cook for 20 minutes and serve.

Nutritional information per serving: Calories: 163, Fat: 0.5g, Sodium: 50mg, Fiber: 4.7g, Sugar: 1g, Carbohydrate: 38g, Protein: 1g.

27. SEASONED FRIED MUSHROOMS

Preparation Time: 15 Minutes

Cooking Time: 15 Minutes

Servings: 10

Ingredients:

- 12 Portobello mushrooms
- Chopped onion – 1 tablespoon
- Garlic powder – 1 teaspoon
- Breadcrumbs – 1 cup
- Salt – 1 pinch
- 1 Egg

Instructions:

1. Take a bowl and mix everything except for egg and panko.
2. Then keep aside.
3. Put egg to another bowl.
4. Breadcrumbs to another bowl.
5. Now dip the mushroom in egg mix.
6. Then in the breadcrumb mix.
7. Place them in the basket.
8. Select air crisp mode.
9. Set the temperature to 370F / 188C and cook for 10 minutes.
10. Then serve when it is reduce the heat.

Nutritional information per serving: Calories: 238, Fat: 18g, Sodium: 282mg, Fiber: 2g, Sugar: 4g, Carbohydrate: 10g, Protein: 7g.

28. SWEET FRIED APPLE CHIPS

Preparation Time: 15 Minutes

Cooking Time: 10 Minutes

Servings: 4

Ingredients:

- 2 Sliced apples
- Cinnamon powder – 1 teaspoon

Instructions:

1. Put the apple slices in to the ninja foodi basket.
2. Then sprinkle the cinnamon powder over the apples.
3. Choose air crisp mode and cook for 10 minutes at 300F / 148C.
4. Once they are done take out and serve.

Nutritional information per serving: Calories: 48, Fat: 1g, Sodium: 3mg, Fiber: 6g, Sugar: 2g, Carbohydrate: 14g, Protein: 1g.

29. SPROUT BITES

Preparation Time: 10 Minutes

Cooking Time: 15 Minutes

Servings: 5

Ingredients:

- Sliced brussels sprouts – 2lb / 907g
- Olive oil – 2 tablespoons
- 1 Squeezed lemon
- Melted butter– 1 ½ tablespoons
- Pepper – 1/8 teaspoon
- Mustard – 1 teaspoon
- Garlic salt - 1 ¼ teaspoon
- Chili powder - ¼ teaspoon

Instructions:

1. Cut the sprouts in half and put in to a bowl.
2. Then add oil, chili powder, garlic salt, lime juice, butter, mustard and sprouts.
3. Then mix them well.
4. Place them in the basket.
5. Select air crisp mode and cook for 15 minutes at 380F / 193C.
6. Let them cool and serve.

Nutritional information per serving: Calories: 184, Fat: 12g, Sodium: 823mg, Fiber: 7g, Sugar: 3g, Carbohydrate: 18g, Protein: 6g.

30. VEGETABLE FRIED RICE

Preparation Time: 10 Minutes

Cooking Time: 10 Minutes

Servings: 6

Ingredients:

- 2 Diced carrots
- 1 Leak stalk (chopped)
- Rice – 1 cup
- 1 Sliced potato
- Salt – ¼ teaspoon
- Olive oil – ½ cup
- ½ a sliced onion
- Water - 1 cup

Instructions:

1. Put water to the cooking pot
2. Then add rice to the pot.
3. Place all the vegetable on the rack.
4. Close the pressure cooking lid and cook for 15 minutes at high pressure.
5. Do a quick pressure release. (refer chapter 3)
6. Take the vegetables and rice out and mix well.
7. Enjoy with some curry or just this dish.

Nutritional information per serving: Calories: 186, Fat: 18g, Sodium: 201mg, Fiber: 2g, Sugar: 1g, Carbohydrate: 5g, Protein: 2g.

CHAPTER 12 – SEAFOOD RECIPES

1. AIR FRIED COD

Preparation Time: 5 Minutes

Cooking Time: 5 Minutes

Servings: 4

Ingredients:

- 2 Cod fillets
- Water – 1 cup
- 3 Lemon wedges
- Rosemary – 5 stalks
- Salt & pepper as required
- Lemon juice - ½ Cup

Instructions:

1. Pour the water and lemon juice to the cooking pot of ninja foodi.
2. Include rosemary as well.
3. Place the cod fillets on the rack. Place the rack in the lower position.
4. Keep the lemon slices on the top of cod fillets.
5. Add salt & pepper as required.
6. Close the pressure cooking lid.
7. Seal the valve and cook for 5 minutes at high pressure.
8. Do a quick release. And carefully open the lid when all pressure goes out.
9. Take the cod fillets out and place in the basket.
10. Select air crisp mode and cook for 8 minutes at 400F / 204C.
11. Let them cool for few minutes.
12. Serve to your table.

Nutritional information per serving: Calories: 274, Fat: 15g, Sodium: 183mg, Fiber: 1g, Sugar: 7g, Carbohydrate: 12g, Protein: 25g.

2. AIR FRIED TUNA FILLETS

Preparation Time: 10 Minutes
Cooking Time: 12 Minutes
Servings: 6
Ingredients:

- Tuna fillets – 2lb / 907g
- Garlic powder – 1 teaspoon
- Pepper – ½ teaspoon
- Chopped parsley – 1 teaspoon
- Sliced butter – 4 tablespoons
- Brown sugar – 3 tablespoons
- Salt – 1 teaspoon

Instructions:

1. Take a bowl and mix all the spices together.
2. Now apply the spices over the fish fillet.
3. Then place butter over fillets.
4. Close air fryer lid and select air crisp mode.
5. Then cook for 12 minutes at 400F / 204C.
6. When it is done serve in a dish.

Nutritional information per serving: Calories: 306, Fat: 18g, Sodium: 524mg, Fiber: 1g, Sugar: 5g, Carbohydrate: 7g, Protein: 30g.

3. AIR FRIED SHRIMPS

Preparation Time: 10 Minutes

Cooking Time: 12 Minutes

Servings: 6

Ingredients:

- Shrimps (peeled) – 15oz / 425g
- Sliced fried sausages – 14oz / 396g
- Diced onion – ¼ cup
- Fish seasoning – 1/8 cup
- Cooking spray
- Steamed potatoes – 4 cups
- 4 Corn cobs

Instructions:

1. Cut the potatoes in half.
2. Add other ingredients to a bowl and mix well with potatoes.
3. Put a parchment paper to the basket of your ninja foodi.
4. Now move the mixture to the basket.
5. Fill ¼ of the basket.
6. Do it in two badges.
7. Select air crisp mode and cook for 8 minutes at 380F / 193C.
8. Once it's done serve.

Nutritional information per serving: Calories: 195, Fat: 1g, Sodium: 580mg, Protein: 48g.

4. CRUNCHY TUNA SLICES

Preparation Time: 5 Minutes
Cooking Time: 12 Minutes
Servings: 2
Ingredients:

- Tuna fillet – 1lb / 454g
- 1 Sliced lemon
- Seasoning – 1 teaspoon
- Butter – ¼ cup
- Salt – 1 teaspoon

- Cooking spray

Instructions:

1. Apply cooking spray over the ninja foodi basket.
2. Now put the tuna fillets in the basket.
3. Then add lemon and butter on the top.
4. Close the air fryer lid and select air crisp mode, then cook at 400F / 204C for 12 minutes.
5. Take them out and serve.

Nutritional information per serving: Calories: 403, Fat: 25g, Sodium: 1485mg, Fiber: 2g, Sugar: 1g, Carbohydrate: 5g, Protein: 42g.

5. CHEESY SHRIMP & TOMATO MIX

Preparation Time: 12 Minutes

Cooking Time: 22 Minutes

Servings: 6

Ingredients:

- Chopped onions – 1½ cups
- Chopped tomatoes – 15oz / 425g
- Butter – 2 tbsp
- Garlic – 1 tbsp
- Red pepper flakes – ½ tsp
- Oregano – 1 tsp
- Salt – 1 tsp

- Shrimps – 1lb / 425g

Instructions:
1. Select the saute mode in your ninja foodi.
2. Add the butter, pepper flakes and garlic to the cooking pot.
3. Then add salt, tomatoes, onions and oregano to the pot.
4. Include the shrimps.
5. Close the pressure cooking lid and select low pressure and cook for 2 minutes.
6. After that do a natural pressure release. (refer chapter 3 for more info)
7. Move the mixture to a dish.
8. Serve with rice or tacos.

Nutritional information per serving: Calories: 212, Fat: 11g, Sodium: 535mg, Fiber: 1g, Sugar: 2g, Carbohydrate: 6g, Protein: 18g.

6. COCONUT MIXED TUNA CURRY

Preparation Time: 5 Minutes
Cooking Time: 15 Minutes
Servings: 3
Ingredients:

- Tuna steaks - 1½ lb / 680g
- 1 Chopped tomato
- 2 Sliced chilies
- Turmeric – ½ teaspoon
- Chili powder– 1 teaspoon
- Coconut Milk – 2 cups
- 2 Sliced onions
- Salt to taste
- Lime juice as required
- Garlic – 2 cloves
- Diced ginger – 1 tablespoon
- 6 Curry leaves
- Coriander – 1 tablespoon
- Cumin – 2 teaspoon

Instructions:

1. Put the ninja foodi on saute mode (medium heat) and put some oil to the cooking pot.
2. Then add curry leaves.
3. Put garlic, onion, ginger and stir fry them for 3 minutes.
4. Now put remaining spices and mix well.

5. Add coconut milk and lets boil for 2 minutes.
6. Now add chilies, fish and tomato pieces.
7. Close the pressure cooking lid.
8. Cook for 5 minutes in low pressure.
9. Do a natural pressure release after the time. Leave it 10 minutes to release the pressure. Open the valve to release remaining pressure. Then open the lid.
10. Add more salt if needed.
11. Serve with rice or noodles.

Nutritional information per serving: Calories: 201, Fat: 8.4g, Sodium: 53mg, Fiber: 1g, Sugar: 3g, Carbohydrate: 7g, Protein: 22g.

7. CHEESE ADDED PRAWN SALAD

Preparation Time: 30 Minutes

Cooking Time: 45 Minutes

Servings: 4

Ingredients:

- Prawns – 1lb / 454g
- Fish seasoning – 1 tablespoon
- Olive oil – 1 teaspoon
- 1 Chopped onion
- Minced garlic – 1 clove
- 1 Chopped red bell pepper
- Chicken broth – ½ cup

- Diced tomatoes – 1 can
- Milk – 1 cup
- Butter – 1 teaspoon
- Shredded cheese – 2oz / 56g
- Corn flour – ½ cup
- Chopped chives – 2 tablespoons
- Whip cream – ¼ cup
- Salt & pepper
- Lime juice – 2 tablespoons
- Tomato sauce – ¼ teaspoon
- Salt – ½ teaspoon
- Black pepper - ¼ teaspoon
- Water – 1 cup

Instructions:

1. Take a bowl and put prawns and fish seasoning. Then mix well.
2. Select saute mode in your ninja foodi.
3. Put olive oil, garlic, onion, bell pepper and stir fry for 3 minutes in medium heat.
4. Stop the saute and add chicken broth, diced tomatoes, lemon juice, tomato sauce, salt, black pepper to the pot.
5. Add water and milk and corn flour to a bowl and add salt and pepper then mix well.
6. Then add the prawns to the mixture.

7. Close the pressure cooking lid and cook for 8 minutes in medium pressure.
8. Do a quick pressure release and open the lid (refer chapter 3).
9. Put the mixture in to a dish.
10. Sprinkle some cheese over top and serve.

Nutritional information per serving: Calories: 365, Fat: 10g, Sodium: 887mg, Fiber: 2.8g, Sugar: 1g, Carbohydrate: 39g, Protein: 37g.

8. FRIED SHRIMP RICE

Preparation Time: 10 Minutes

Cooking Time: 45 Minutes

Servings: 4

Ingredients:

- Shrimp – 5oz / 141g
- Crab meat – 5oz / 141g
- Coriander – 1 bunch
- Parsley – 1 stalk
- Salt & pepper
- ½ a green pepper
- ½ a red pepper

- Chopped fish – 5 oz / 141g
- Cooked rice – 1 ½ cup
- 2 Chopped onions
- Water – 1 ½ cups
- Garlic – 3 cloves
- 3 Tomatoes
- Olive oil – 2 teaspoons

Instructions:

1. Put olive oil in to the cooking pot.
2. Put all the spices.
3. Then add prawns, carbs, and fish.
4. Select the saute mode and stir cook for 10 minutes in high heat.
5. Then add the rice to it.
6. Mix everything well.
7. Turn off the heat.
8. Put in to the keep warm and close the air fryer lid.
9. Keep like that for 15 minutes.
10. Open the lid and serve.

Nutritional information per serving: Calories: 411, Fat: 15g, Sodium: 580mg, Fiber: 5g, Sugar: 1g, Carbohydrate: 36g, Protein: 33g.

9. FRIED BATTERED SHRIMPS

Preparation Time: 10 Minutes

Cooking Time: 20 Minutes

Servings: 3

Ingredients:

- Shrimps – 1lb / 454g
- Salt & pepper
- Olive oil spray
- Chili sauce
- Breadcrumbs – ¾ cup
- Paprika
- 1 Egg
- Flour – ½ cup
- Chicken seasoning

Instructions:

1. Take a bowl and add shrimps and seasonings.
2. Mix them well.
3. Take 3 more bowls.
4. Put egg to one.
5. Put flour to one.
6. Put breadcrumbs to one.
7. Then dip shrimps in flour, eggs then breadcrumbs.
8. Place in the basket.
9. Apply some olive oil spray over them.
10. Select air crisp mode and cook for 5 minutes at 400F / 204C.
11. Take them out and serve.

Nutritional information per serving: Calories: 192, Fat: 10g, Sodium: 812mg, Fiber: 1g, Carbohydrate: 10g, Protein: 15g

10. GRILLED PRAWNS

Preparation Time: 10 Minutes
Cooking Time: 15 Minutes
Servings: 4
Ingredients:

- Prawns – 12oz / 340g
- Fish seasoning
- Cooking spray
- Mixed vegetables 12oz / 340g

Instructions:

1. Take bowl and mix everything well.
2. Move the mixture equally to two aluminum sheets.
3. Fold them and place in the rack.
4. Close the air fryer lid select grill function.
5. Select high and cook for 15 minutes.
6. Serve with rice.

Nutritional information per serving: Calories: 58, Sodium: 135mg, Fiber: 4g, Sugar: 2g, Carbohydrate: 12g, Protein: 4g.

11. GARLIC PRAWNS

Preparation Time: 10 Minutes

Cooking Time: 20 Minutes

Servings: 5

Ingredients:

- Soy Sauce - ½ cup
- Cornstarch – 2tbsp
- Prawns - 15oz / 425g
- Mixed vegetables – 15oz / 425g
- Tomato sauce – 2 tbsp
- Garlic – 1 clove
- Ginger – 1 tsp

Instructions:

1. Put the ninja foodi to saute mode and add soy sauce, tomato sauce, ginger and garlic to the cooking pot.
2. Then add shrimps and vegetables to the mixture.
3. Mix well them.
4. Close the air fryer lid and cook for 10 minutes at 350F / 177C.
5. Then serve the dish.

Nutritional information per serving: Calories: 137, Fat: 12g, Sodium: 46mg, Fiber: 2g, Sugar: 3g, Carbohydrate: 18g, Protein: 38g.

12. HOT SALTY FRIED FISH

Preparation Time: 1 Minutes
Cooking Time: 5 Minutes
Servings: 2
Ingredients:

- Salmon slices – 8oz / 227g
- Salt – ¼ teaspoon
- Paprika – ¼ teaspoon
- Olive oil – 2 tablespoons
- Butter - 1 tablespoon
- Black pepper – ¼ teaspoon

Instructions:

1. Apply olive oil over the fish.
2. Rub seasonings on the fish slices.
3. Place the fish in the basket of ninja foodi.
4. Select the air crisp function.
5. Cook at 380F / 193C for 10 minutes.
6. Once it is done put the butter on the top of fish.
7. Wait till it melts and serve.

Nutritional information per serving: Calories: 338, Fat: 9g, Sodium: 391mg, Fiber: 1g, Sugar: 1g, Carbohydrate: 2g, Protein: 24g.

13. LOBSTER SOUP

Preparation Time: 10 Minutes

Cooking Time: 10 Minutes

Servings: 3

Ingredients:

- Sliced carrots – 1 cup
- Sliced celery – 1 cup
- Diced tomatoes – 30oz / 850g
- Dried dill – 1 teaspoon
- Black pepper – 1 teaspoon
- Paprika – 5 teaspoon
- 4 Lobster Tails
- Whipping cream – ½ cup
- 2 Minced green onion

- Minced garlic– 1 clove
- Butter – 1 tablespoon
- Chicken broth – 30oz / 850ml
- Old bay seasoning - 1 tablespoon

Instructions:
1. Take a bowl add green onion, butter and garlic and mix well.
2. Add carrots and tomatoes and mix more.
3. Put the mixture to the cooking pot of ninja foodi.
4. Then add the chicken broth and spices to it as well.
5. Put the lobster tails to the pot as well.
6. Close the pressure cooking lid and cook for 5 minutes at high pressure.
7. Then let naturally release the pressure.
8. Open the valve to let go any remaining pressure and open the lid.
9. Then add some whip cream and stir well.
10. Then serve in a soup bowl.

Nutritional information per serving: Calories: 373, Fat: 31g, Sodium: 770mg, Fiber: 1g, Sugar: 3g, Carbohydrate: 15g, Protein: 8g.

14. LEMON FLAVORED TUNA BITES

Preparation Time: 5 Minutes

Cooking Time: 10 Minutes

Servings: 3

Ingredients:

- Water – ¾ cup
- Salt & pepper
- ½ a sliced lemon
- 1 Sliced zucchini
- 1 Sliced bell pepper
- 2 Sliced carrots
- One stalk of dill, parsley, basil
- Tuna slice (cut in to small pieces) – 1½ lb / 680g
- Ghee – 2 tablespoon

Instructions:

1. Put herbs and water to the cooking pot of ninja foodi.
2. Now put tuna in to a bowl.
3. Place the rack inside the pot.
4. Keep fish slices on it.
5. Add salt, pepper, ghee, and place lemon slices on the top.
6. Close the pressure cooker lid and set high pressure.
7. Cook for 5 minutes.
8. Do a quick pressure release once cooking is done.
9. Move the fish in to a plate.
10. Remove the water.
11. Put the vegetable to the pot.
12. Add ghee and lemon juice.
13. Choose the saute mode and cook for 5 minutes at high heat.
14. Stir occasionally.
15. Serve tuna with fried vegetables.

Nutritional information per serving: Calories: 345, Fat: 20g, Sodium: 280mg, Fiber: 3g, Sugar: 5g, Carbohydrate: 8g, Protein: 30g.

15. MIX SALMON STEW

Preparation Time: 15 Minutes

Cooking Time: 3 Hours

Servings: 6

Ingredients:

- Chopped tomatoes – 28oz / 794g
- Vegetable broth – 4 cups
- Celery – ½ tsp
- Red pepper flakes – ¼ tsp
- Cayenne pepper – 1/8 tsp
- Salt & pepper
- Shredded salmon - 2lb / 907g
- Chopped parsley – 2 tbsp
- Minced garlic – 3 cloves
- Cubed potatoes – 1lb / 454g
- Chopped onion – ½ cup
- Thyme – 1 tsp
- Basil – 1 tsp
- Oregano – 1 tsp

Instructions:

1. Put all the ingredients to the ninja foodi cooking pot. Not the salmon.
2. Select slow cook function.
3. Cook for 2 hours and 15 minutes. (close the pressure cooking lid)

4. Then add fish and cook for another 30 minutes.
5. Top with parsley and serve.

Nutritional information per serving: Calories: 112, Fat: 1g, Sodium: 1330mg, Fiber: 4g, Sugar: 5g, Carbohydrate: 20g, Protein: 7g.

16. PRAWN NOODLES

Preparation Time: Minutes

Cooking Time: Minutes

Servings:

Ingredients:

- Noodles – 1lb / 454g
- Juice and zest of 1 lemon
- Salt
- Pepper powder
- Parsley
- Parmesan cheese
- Butter - 1 stick
- Prawns – 15oz / 425g

- Water - 3cups
- Chopped garlic – 5 cloves
- Olive oil

Instructions:
1. Put prawns, garlic, butter and lemon juice to a cooking pot and select saute mode.
2. Do it for 2 minutes and stop saute.
3. Clean the pot and add water.
4. Then noodles, salt, olive oil and close the pressure cooking lid.
5. Cook for 7 minutes at high pressure.
6. Quick release the pressure and open the lid.
7. Add the prawns back to noodles and mix well.
8. Serve with parsley and parmesan cheese.

Nutritional information per serving: Calories: 341, Fat: 7g, Sodium: 325mg, Fiber: 8g, Sugar: 5g, Carbohydrate: 34g, Protein: 35g.

17. PRESSURE COOKED SALMON

Preparation Time: 5 Minutes

Cooking Time: 5 Minutes

Servings: 4

Ingredients:

- 3 Limes
- Water – ¾ cup
- 4 Salmon fillets
- Butter - 1 tbsp
- Salt – ¼ tsp
- Pepper powder – ¼ tsp
- Dill – 1 bunch

Instructions:

1. Put lime juice. Water, to the cooking pot.
2. Form the rack.
3. Put the salmon fillets on to the rack.
4. Now sprinkle the dill over the fish.
5. Apply lime juice on fillets as well.
6. Close the pressure cooking lid.
7. Cook for 5 minutes at high pressure.
8. Quickly release the pressure and serve with salt and pepper.

Nutritional information per serving: Calories: 443, Fat: 30g, Sodium: 405mg, Fiber: 4g, Sugar: 3g, Carbohydrate: 13g, Protein: 36g.

18. PEPPER SPICED SHRIMP RICE

Preparation Time: 10 Minutes

Cooking Time: 5 Minutes

Servings: 5

Ingredients:

- Shrimps – 1lb / 454g
- Rice – 1 cup
- Butter – 4 tablespoon
- Powdered pepper – ¼ teaspoon
- Red pepper flakes – ¼ teaspoon
- 1 Chopped onion
- Chopped garlic – 4 cloves

- 1 Chopped red pepper
- Chicken broth – 1 cup
- Turmeric – 1 teaspoon
- Salt – ½ teaspoon

Instructions:
1. Select saute mode and put butter and garlic then cook.
2. Then add salt, turmeric, pepper, pepper flakes and cook.
3. Include rice and stir cook.
4. Add chicken broth and prawns.
5. Close the pressure cooking lid and cook for 10 minutes in high pressure.
6. When it is done do a quick release and open the lid and serve.

Nutritional information per serving: Calories: 318, Fat: 16g, Sodium: 1356mg, Fiber: 4g, Sugar: 3g, Carbohydrate: 15g, Protein: 45g.

19. PRESSURE COOKED CRAB LEGS

Preparation Time: 5 Minutes

Cooking Time: 15 Minutes

Servings: 5

Ingredients:

- Water – 1½ cups
- One lime juice
- Melted butter – 1/3 cup
- Crab legs– 2lb / 907g

Instructions:

1. Put water to the cooking pot.
2. Add carbs to the pot.
3. Close pressure cooking lid and cook for 10 minutes at high pressure.

4. Quick release the pressure and open the lid.
5. Serve with butter and lime juice.

Nutritional information per serving: Calories: 198, Fat: 15g, Sodium: 325mg, Carbohydrate: 1.3g, Protein: 13g.

20. TILAPIA TACOS

Preparation Time: 10 Minutes
Cooking Time: 17 Minutes
Servings: 8
Ingredients:
- 4 Tilapia fillets
- Paprika – 1 teaspoon
- Pepper - ½ teaspoon

- 8 Tortillas
- Salt - ½ teaspoon
- Olive oil

Instructions:

1. Put fillets in to a bowl and add salt, pepper and paprika.
2. Mix them well.
3. Apply oil in the basket.
4. Put the fish slices in to the basket.
5. Select air crisp mode and cook for 10 minutes at 360F / 182C.
6. Take out the fish when it is done.
7. Then apply olive oil over the tortillas and put in the basket.
8. Cook for another 5 minutes at 360F / 182C.
9. Serve with fish.

Nutritional information per serving: Calories: 214, Fat: 5g, Sodium: 237mg, Fiber: 22g, Sugar: 2g, Carbohydrate: 24g, Protein: 25g.

21. SEASONED LOBSTER

Preparation Time: 3 Minutes

Cooking Time: 5 Minutes

Servings: 2

Ingredients:

- 2 Lobster Tails
- Butter – 4 tablespoons
- Parsley – 1 teaspoon
- Salt & pepper
- Chopped garlic – 1 clove

Instructions:

1. Cut the lobster tail in the middle and take some crab meat out from fingers.
2. Place them inside the ninja foodi basket and select grill function.
3. Set the heat to high and keep it ready.
4. Meanwhile take bowl and put butter, parsley, garlic. Then mix well.
5. Apply the butter mix over lobster tails.
6. Apply olive oil in the basket and keep the lobster tail in the basket.
7. Then grill for 5 minutes in high heat.
8. Take them out and serve once they reduce heat.

Nutritional information per serving: Calories: 450, Fat: 25g, Sodium: 537mg, Carbohydrate: 5g, Protein: 46g.

22. SIMPLY FRIED PRAWNS

Preparation Time: 5 Minutes

Cooking Time: 10 Minutes

Servings: 5

Ingredients:

- Prawns – 1lb / 454g
- Salt & pepper
- Lemon juice – 1 tbsp
- Breadcrumbs – ½ cup
- 1 Egg
- Whole wheat bread

Instructions:
1. Take a bowl and add prawns.
2. Add salt, pepper and lime juice.

3. Put egg and breadcrumbs to separate bowls.
4. Mix well and let it marinate.
5. Then take prawns and dip in the egg bowl.
6. Then the breadcrumb bowl.
7. Keep inside the basket.
8. Spray cooking oil and close the air fryer lid.
9. Select air crisp mode.
10. Cook for 10 minutes at 380F / 193C.
11. Serve with bread slices.

Nutritional information per serving: Calories: 247, Fat: 11g, Sodium: 351mg, Fiber: 3g, Sugar: 1g, Carbohydrate: 23g, Protein: 42g.

23. STEMED CRABS

Preparation Time: Minutes

Cooking Time: Minutes

Servings:

Ingredients:

- Water – 1 ½ cups
- Old bay seasoning – 1 tablespoon
- Crabs - 1½ lb / 680g
- Garlic butter

Instructions:

1. First you have to clean the crabs and remove the dirt inside them.
2. Then put crabs in to bowl and add old bay seasoning.

3. Mix them well.
4. Take rack and place it the low position.
5. Then place crabs on it.
6. Put some water in to the cooking pot.
7. Close the pressure cooking lid.
8. Select pressure and cook for 5 minutes in high pressure.
9. Do a quick pressure release and take the crabs out.
10. Serve with the garlic butter.

Nutritional information per serving: Calories: 789, Fat: 11g, Sodium: 5468mg, Carbohydrate: 3g, Protein: 186g.

24. STEAMED FISH & POTATOES

Preparation Time: 10 Minutes

Cooking Time: 15 Minutes

Servings: 3

Ingredients:

- 3 Tilapia fillets
- 3 Sliced potatoes
- Salt - 3 teaspoons
- Lemon juice – 1 tablespoon
- Pepper powder 1½ teaspoons
- Soy sauce – 2 tablespoons
- Water – 2½ cups

Instructions:

1. Put the water in to the cooking pot.
2. Then add the sliced potatoes.
3. Meanwhile take a bowl and add salt, tilapia fillets, pepper and lemon juice.
4. Mix well and let it marinate.
5. After 10 minutes place the fish fillets on the rack.
6. Close the pressure cooking lid.
7. Select pressure and cook for 10 minutes in high pressure.
8. Do a quick pressure release and open the lid. (refer chapter 3)
9. Take fish and potato slices out.
10. Remove the water.
11. Place potatoes and fish in to the basket and sprinkle some soy sauce.
12. Close the air fryer lid and select air crisp mode then cook for 5 minutes at 400F / 204C.
13. Take them out and serve to the table.

Nutritional information per serving: Calories: 285, Fat: 15g, Sodium: 1050mg, Fiber: 6g, Sugar: 3g, Carbohydrate: 37g, Protein: 56g.

25. STEAMED PRAWNS WITH CARROTS

Preparation Time: 15 Minutes
Cooking Time: 45 Minutes
Servings: 4
Ingredients:

- Prawns – 1lb / 454g
- Fried diced bacon – 3 strips
- Chopped onion – 1/3 cup
- Chopped bell peppers– ½ cup
- Minced garlic – 1 tablespoon
- Sliced carrots – ½ lb / 227g
- Chicken broth – ¼ cup
- Hot sauce– ¼ teaspoon
- Corn flour – ½ cup
- Salt – ½ teaspoon
- Pepper powder – ¼ teaspoon
- Whip cream – ¼ cup
- Diced tomatoes - 1½ cups
- Lime juice - 2 tablespoons

Instructions:

1. Select saute mode and put onions and bell peppers to the cooking pot.
2. Cook for 3 minutes.
3. Include garlic and stir it.
4. Stop the saute mode.

5. Mix tomatoes, chicken broth, lemon juice, pepper, salt, corn flour and hot sauce.
6. Mix everything well.
7. Then add carrots and prawns to the cooking pot.
8. Close the pressure cooking lid.
9. Cook in high pressure for 10 minutes.
10. Release pressure naturally and remove remaining pressure from valve.
11. Then open the lid and serve.

Nutritional information per serving: Calories: 294, Fat: 8g, Sodium: 1176mg, Fiber: 3g, Sugar: 8g, Carbohydrate: 18g, Protein: 29g.

26. SHRIMP & MACARONI

Preparation Time: 5 Minutes

Cooking Time: 20 Minutes

Servings: 5

Ingredients:

- Shrimps – 2lb / 907g
- Olive oil – 2 tablespoons
- Chicken stock – ½ cup
- Cooked macaroni – 1 pack
- Lime juice – 1 tablespoons
- Salt & pepper
- Butter – 2 tablespoons

- Minced garlic– 1 tablespoon

Instructions:

1. Put oil and butter to the cooking pot.
2. Select saute mode and medium heat.
3. Then add garlic, chicken stock and stir cook.
4. Stop the saute and add shrimps. Then close the lid.
5. Add cooked macaroni to the pot and mix well.
6. Then serve the dish.

Nutritional information per serving: Calories: 223, Fat: 13.5g, Sodium: 556mg, Fiber: 0.3g, Sugar: 1g, Carbohydrate: 4.1g, Protein: 22.8g.

27. TUNA NOODLE SOUP

Preparation Time: 5 Minutes

Cooking Time: 15 Minutes

Servings: 3

Ingredients:

- Diced onion – 2/3 cup
- Minced garlic – 2 cloves
- Noodles – 10oz / 283g
- Diced bacon – 2 strips
- Salmon – 14oz / 397g
- Mixed vegetables – 1 pack
- Vegetable broth – 2 cups
- Pepper powder – 1 tsp
- Spinach – 1 cup

Instructions:

1. Select saute mode and add onions, garlic, bacon, and cook for 4 minutes under high heat.
2. Stop the saute mode.
3. Add salmon, vegetables, pasta, broth and spices.
4. Then mix well.
5. Close the pressure cooking lid and select pressure and cook for 5 minutes at high pressure.
6. When it is completed do a quick pressure release and mix spinach with it and serve.

Nutritional information per serving: Calories: 214, Fat: 8.6g, Sodium: 400mg, Fiber: 0.8g, Sugar: 1.5g, Carbohydrate: 3g, Protein: 35g.

28. SPICY SALMON

Preparation Time: 10 Minutes
Cooking Time: 25 Minutes
Servings: 2
Ingredients:

- Fish sauce – 2 tbsp
- Vegetable broth – 1 cup
- Salmon slice – 12oz / 340g
- Coconut milk – 1 cup
- Diced tomato – ½ cup

- Salt – ½ tsp
- Powdered pepper – ¼ tsp
- Broccoli - 1 ½ cups
- Chopped kale – 1 cup
- Olive oil – 1 tbsp
- 2 Diced onions
- Garlic powder – 1 tsp

Instructions:
1. Add olive oil to the pot.
2. Then onions, garlic powder and select saute mode and cook for 1 minute.
3. Include fish sauce and tomato cook for another 2 minutes.
4. Now put vegetable broth.
5. Close the pressure cooking lid and cook for 15 minutes in high pressure.
6. Do a natural pressure release and open the lid carefully after 20 minutes. (Refer chapter 3 for more).
7. Serve with salt and pepper.

Nutritional information per serving: Calories: 653, Fat: 50g, Sodium: 2045mg, Carbohydrate: 17g, Protein: 37g.

29. SEAFOOD SOUP

Preparation Time: 10 Minutes

Cooking Time: 12 Minutes

Servings: 2

Ingredients:

- Noodles – 4oz / 113g
- Mushrooms – 3oz / 85g
- Vegetable broth – 4 cups
- Prawns and tuna – 10oz / 283g
- Sliced onion – 1 stalk
- Water – 4 cups

Instructions:

1. Take bowl and add water & noodles.
2. In another bowl add broth, vegetables, prawns and tuna.
3. Select saute mode and put both bowls to cooking pot.
4. Cook for 10 minutes and serve the soup.

Nutritional information per serving: Calories: 495, Fat: 5g, Sodium: 3225mg, Fiber: 12g, Sugar: 15g, Carbohydrate: 80g, Protein: 43g.

30. SALMON CAKES

Preparation Time: 12 Minutes
Cooking Time: 10 Minutes
Servings: 4
Ingredients:

- 2 Salmon slices (chopped)
- Breadcrumbs – ¼ cup
- Shredded parmesan – 1oz / 28g
- Powdered pepper – 1 teaspoon
- Garlic powder – ½ teaspoon
- Shredded cheddar – 1oz / 28g
- 1 Egg
- Hot sauce – 2 tablespoon
- Onion powder – ½ teaspoon

Instructions:

1. Take a bowl and mix all the ingredients.
2. Make medium sized patties from hand.
3. Place the patties in the basket.
4. Select air crisp mode and apply some oil over them.
5. Cook at 400F /204C for 12 minutes.
6. Then serve the meal.

Nutritional information per serving: Calories: 173, Fat: 7g, Carbohydrate: 12g, Protein: 18g.

CHAPTER 13

MEAT & POULTRY RECIPES

1. AIR FRIED RIBS

Preparation Time: 10 Minutes

Cooking Time: 1 Hour

Servings: 4

Ingredients:

- Water – ½ cup
- BBQ sauce - 2 cups
- Seasoned back ribs – 1 rack

Instructions:

1. Put the water in the cooking pot of ninja foodi.
2. Slice the ribs in to 4 parts.
3. Apply some cooking spray over the basket.
4. Apply BBQ sauce over the ribs from a brush.
5. Close the pressure cooking lid.
6. Cook for 35 minutes in high pressure.
7. Release the steam quickly.
8. Remove the pressure cooking lid and close the fixed air fryer lid.
9. Select air crisp function and cook for 15 minutes at 400F / 204C.
10. Serve when they reduce the heat.

Nutritional information per serving: Calories: 328, Fat: 12g, Sodium: 1103mg, Fiber: 1g, Sugar: 24g, Carbohydrate: 43g, Protein: 12g.

2. AIR FRYED CHICKEN

Preparation Time: 10 Minutes
Cooking Time: 30 Minutes
Servings: 5
Ingredients:

- Chicken – 3lb / 1.36kg
- Water – 1 cup
- Salt – 1 teaspoon
- Butter – 2 tablespoons
- Paprika - 1 teaspoon
- Garlic powder – 1 teaspoon
- Onion powder – ½ teaspoon
- Garlic butter 2 tablespoons
- Flour – ¼ cup
- Chicken broth – 2 cup
- Salt & pepper

Instructions:
1. Take the chicken and place on a cutting board.
2. Then open it and apply pepper, paprika, salt, garlic and onion powder inside the chicken.

3. Put the chicken inside the air fryer basket.
4. Add the chicken broth to the cooking pot.
5. Close the pressure lid and cook for 15 minutes at high pressure.
6. Preform a quick release when it is completed. (Check chapter 3).
7. Discard the liquid in the pot.
8. Apply garlic butter on the chicken.
9. Keep basket again in the ninja foodi and close the air fryer lid.
10. Choose air crisp mode and cook for 15 minutes at 400F / 204C.
11. Take it out and serve.

Nutritional information per serving: Calories: 540, Fat: 32g, Sodium: 1015mg, Fiber: 1g, Sugar: 2g, Carbohydrate: 12g, Protein: 46g.

3. AIR FRIED BEEF LOAF

Preparation Time: 15 Minutes

Cooking Time: 25 Minutes

Servings: 4

Ingredients:

- Ground beef – 1lb / 454g
- ½ a diced bell pepper
- Breadcrumbs – 1/3 cup
- Sliced onions – ½ cup
- Chopped parsley – 1 tbsp
- Minced garlic – 1 clove
- 1 Egg
- Salt – ½ tsp
- Tomato sauce
- Milk – 2 tbsp
- Shredded parmesan – 2 tbsp

Instructions:

1. Take a bowl and mix all the ingredients well (except tomato sauce).
2. Create 2-3 loaves from the mixture.
3. Place in the basket and close the air fryer lid.
4. Select air crisp mode and cook for 20 minutes at 380F / 193C.
5. Serve with tomato sauce.

Nutritional information per serving: Calories: 345, Fat: 20g, Sodium: 708mg, Fiber: 2g, Sugar: 1g, Carbohydrate: 15g, Protein: 25g.

4. AIR FRIED BEEF SLICES

Preparation Time: 10 Minutes
Cooking Time: 55 Minutes
Servings: 8
Ingredients:
- Slice beef – 2lb / 907g
- 2 tbsp butter – 2 tablespoons
- Minced garlic – 3 tablespoons
- Beef stock – 1 cup
- Salt – ½ teaspoon

- Pepper – ¼ teaspoon
- Garlic salt – 1 teaspoon
- 4 Carrots (sliced in to chunks)
- 4 Sliced tomatoes
- Chili sauce – 2 tablespoon
- 2 tbsp olive oil – 2 tablespoons
- 1 Sliced onion

Instructions:
1. Select saute mode and put butter and oil.
2. Then add beef, pepper and salt.
3. When the beef cooked for about 2 minutes stop the saute function.
4. Put onions, garlic, chili sauce and broth to the pot.
5. Close pressure cooker lid and cook for 40 minute at low pressure.
6. Do a natural pressure release. (refer chapter 3).
7. Open the pressure valve before opening the lid.
8. Then put vegetables.
9. Close the pressure lid and cook another 5 minutes in high pressure.
10. Do a quick release.
11. Select air crisp mode and close the air frying lid.
12. Put the beef and veggies in the basket and cook for 10 minutes at 380F / 193C.
13. Take them out and serve the meal.

Nutritional information per serving: Calories: 552, Fat: 33g, Sodium: 792mg, Fiber: 5g, Sugar: 1g, Carbohydrate: 20g, Protein: 48g.

5. AIR FRYED TURKEY BREAST

Preparation Time: 15 Minutes
Cooking Time: 50 Minutes
Servings: 5
Ingredients:

- Turkey breast – 3lb / 1.36kg
- Minced parsley – 2 tsp
- Paprika – 1 tsp

- Salt – 1 tsp
- Chopped pepper – 1 tsp
- Rosemary – ½ tsp
- Butter – 4 tbsp
- Olive oil – 1 tbsp
- Lime juice – 1 tbsp
- Minced garlic – 1 clove

Instructions:

1. Put the turkey on a cutting board.
2. Take bowl and add other ingredients and mix well.
3. Apply the mixture on turkey.
4. Move the turkey in to the basket and close the air fryer lid.
5. Select air crisp mode and cook for 20 minutes at 350F / 177C.
6. During half time turn the turkey the other side and cook.
7. Take the turkey out and slice and serve.

Nutritional information per serving: Calories: 975, Fat: 26g, Sodium: 1184mg, Carbohydrate: 3g, Protein: 175g.

6. PRESSURE COOKED DEVILLED CHICKEN

Preparation Time: 15 Minutes

Cooking Time: 10 Minutes

Servings: 6

Ingredients:

- Diced chicken - 2lb / 907g
- Soy sauce – ¾ cup
- 1 Sliced tomato
- Chicken broth – 1 cup
- 1 Sliced bell pepper

Instructions:

1. Cut chicken in to small pieces.
2. Dip in the soy sauce.
3. Place in the ninja foodi cooking pot.
4. Put tomato and pepper in the pot as well.
5. Close the pressure cooking lid.
6. Cook for 15 minutes in high pressure.
7. Quickly release the pressure and open the lid.
8. Take them out and serve.

Nutritional information per serving: Calories: 283, Fat: 18g, Sodium: 1465mg, Fiber: 1g, Sugar: 4g, Carbohydrate: 5g, Protein: 20g.

7. BEEF CUBES

Preparation Time: 5 Minutes
Cooking Time: 5 Minutes
Servings: 4
Ingredients:

- 4 Beef slices (cut in to cubes)
- Teriyaki sauce – 6oz / 170ml

Instructions:

1. Take a bowl and put beef cubes and teriyaki sauce.
2. Let it marinate for 2 hours.
3. Select air fry mode in your ninja foodi.

4. Place the beef cubes in the basket.
5. Close the air fryer lid and cook for 5 minutes at 390F / 198C under air crisp mode.
6. Take the out and serve.

Nutritional information per serving: Calories: 45, Fat: 3g, Sodium: 835mg, Fiber: 1g, Sugar: 4g, Carbohydrate: 8g, Protein: 5g.

8. BATTER FRIED CHICKEN CRISPIES

Preparation Time: 10 Minutes

Cooking Time: 15 Minutes

Servings: 4

Ingredients:

- Chicken breasts – 5oz / 140g
- Breadcrumbs – ¼ cup
- Oregano – ¼ tsp
- Garlic powder – 1/8 tsp
- Cooking spray
- Salt & pepper
- Paprika – 1.8 tsp

Instructions:

1. Take a bowl and put oregano, paprika, garlic powder and breadcrumbs.
2. Apply cooking spray on the chicken.
3. Rub the breadcrumbs mixture over the chicken.
4. Put them in to the basket.
5. Choose air crisp mode and cook for 5 minutes at 380F / 193C.
6. Serve when it is done.

Nutritional information per serving: Calories: 223, Fat: 5g, Sodium: 245mg, Carbohydrate: 5g, Protein: 38g.

9. BEEF RIBS WITH MAPLE SYRUP

Preparation Time: 15 Minutes

Cooking Time: 55 Minutes

Servings: 6

Ingredients:

- Beef rib – 1 rack (3lb/ 1.36kg)
- Rosemary – 1 tbsp
- BBQ sauce – 1 cup
- Maple syrup – 1 ½ cup

Instructions:

1. Add water in to the pot.
2. Cut the ribs and place in the pot.
3. Put maple syrup and rosemary to the pot.

4. Close the pressure cooking lid and cook for 30 minutes in high pressure.
5. Do a quick pressure release and open the lid.
6. Move the beef pieces in to the basket and close the air fryer lid.
7. Select air crisp function and cook for 15 minutes at 400F / 204C.
8. Once it is done serve the dish.

Nutritional information per serving: Calories: 483, Fat: 10g, Sodium: 227mg, Fiber: 0.5g, Sugar: 1g, Carbohydrate: 30g, Protein: 23g.

10. CRISPY CHICKEN WINGS

Preparation Time: 5 Minutes

Cooking Time: 35 Minutes

Servings: 5

Ingredients:

- Chicken wings – 2lb / 907g
- Chili sauce – 1 cup
- Butter – 1 stick
- Water – 1 cup

Instructions:

1. Add the water in to the cooking pot.
2. Put the chicken wings in the basket.
3. Close the pressure lid and cook for 10 minutes at high pressure.
4. Perform a quick pressure release. (Refer chapter 3).

5. Remove the pressure lid and close the air fryer lid and select air crisp mode.
6. Cook for 20 minutes at 400F / 204C.
7. Take a bowl and add butter and sauce.
8. Mix well and pour over the chicken wings and serve.

Nutritional information per serving: Calories: 187, Fat: 13g, Sodium: 395mg, Carbohydrate: 3g, Protein: 14g.

11. CHEESY CRISPY WINGS

Preparation Time: 10 Minutes

Cooking Time: 15 Minutes

Servings: 4

Ingredients:

- Chicken wings – 2lb / 907g
- Cooking spray
- Salt & pepper as required
- Shredded cheese – ½ cup
- Breadcrumbs – ¾ cup
- 1 Egg

Instructions:

1. Season the chicken with salt, cheese and pepper.
2. Then apply egg mixture and breadcrumbs over them.

3. Place them in the basket and apply cooking spray over them.
4. Choose air crisp mode and cook for 15 minutes at 350F / 177C.
5. Serve when it is done.

Nutritional information per serving: Calories: 328, Fat: 22g, Sodium: 280mg, Carbohydrate: 3g, Protein: 26g.

12. CINNAMON PORK SLICES

Preparation Time: 10 Minutes
Cooking Time: 45 Minutes
Servings: 8
Ingredients:

- 2 Pork slices
- Olive oil – 2 tablespoons
- Black pepper – 1 teaspoon
- Oregano – 1 teaspoon
- Cinnamon – ½ teaspoon
- Cumin – 1 tablespoon
- Salt – 2 teaspoons

Side ingredients,

- 1 Sliced onion
- 1 Sliced Orange
- Crushed cilantro – 2 teaspoons

- Chicken broth – ½ cup
- Chopped garlic – 2 cloves

Instructions:

1. Take bowl and put pork slices.
2. Add olive oil and spices. Then mix well with pork.
3. Put the pork slices in the cooking pot.
4. Select saute mode and set high heat.
5. Cook for 2 minutes.
6. Put side ingredients to the pot.
7. Mix well with the pork slices.
8. Close the pressure cooking lid.
9. Pressure cook for 15 minutes at high pressure.
10. Quickly release the pressure.
11. Remove the pressure lid and close the air fryer lid and use saute mode again till it reduces the liquid inside the pot.
12. Then serve the dish.

Nutritional information per serving: Calories: 165, Fat: 6g, Sodium: 1486mg, Carbohydrate: 5g, Protein: 24g

13. CHICKEN BALLLS

Preparation Time: 15 Minutes

Cooking Time: 8 Minutes

Servings: 2

Ingredients:

- Ground chicken – ½ lb / 227g
- Flour – ½ cup
- 2 Eggs
- Olive oil
- Breadcrumbs – 1 cup
- Garlic powder – 1 teaspoon
- Salt - 1 teaspoon
- Pepper – ¼ teaspoon

Instructions:

1. Take bowl and put garlic powder, breadcrumbs, pepper and salt.
2. Mix them well.
3. Take another bowl and put eggs.
4. In the 3rd bowl put flour.
5. Put salt and pepper in to chicken and mix well.
6. Then dip in flour, then eggs and finally in the breadcrumbs.
7. Apply oil in the basket of ninja foodi.
8. Place the chicken balls in the basket.
9. Close the air fryer lid.
10. Select air crisp mode and cook for 8 minutes at 400F / 204C.
11. Serve when it is done.

Nutritional information per serving: Calories: 495, Fat: 12g, Sodium: 1645mg, Fiber: 3g, Sugar: 1g, Carbohydrate: 48g, Protein: 50g.

14. CHEESE MIXED CHICKEN BREAST

Preparation Time: 15 Minutes
Cooking Time: 20 Minutes
Servings: 6
Ingredients:

- 3 Chicken breasts slices
- Cumin – 1 teaspoon
- Bacon - 6 strips
- Salt and pepper
- Cream cheese – ¾ cup
- Cheddar cheese – ½ cup

Instructions:

1. Put chicken slices in to a bowl and add salt and pepper.
2. Take another bowl and put cream cheese, cheddar cheese and cumin and mix well.
3. Combine both mixture and mix well.
4. Place the chicken slices in the basket and close the air fryer lid.
5. Choose air crisp mode and cook for 25 minutes at 340F / 171C.
6. Serve when they reduced the heat.

Nutritional information per serving: Calories: 406, Fat: 28g, Sodium: 500mg, Fiber: 1g, Sugar: 1g, Carbohydrate: 3g, Protein: 33g.

15. CHICKEN KABOBS

Preparation Time: 15 Minutes

Cooking Time: 18 Minutes

Servings: 6

Ingredients:

- 1 Sliced zucchini
- Chicken cut in to small pieces - ½ lb / 227g
- 1 Onion cut in to large pieces
- Juice of 1 lime
- Olive oil – ¼ cup
- Small tomatoes – 1½ cup
- Minced garlic – 1 clove

-

Instructions:

1. Take a bowl and add garlic, lime juice and olive oil. Mix well.
2. Then add chicken pieces to the bowl and mix further.
3. Let season for 1 night.
4. Take the skewers and put chicken, onion, zucchini, tomato through it.
5. Place them in the basket of ninja foodi and apply some olive oil over them.
6. Select air crisp mode and cook for 15 minutes at 380F / 193C.
7. Serve when it is done.

Nutritional information per serving: Calories: 212, Fat: 14g, Sodium: 95mg, Fiber: 2g, Sugar: 3g, Carbohydrate: 6g, Protein: 18g.

16. CHEESE MIXED GARLIC CHICKEN

Preparation Time: 10 Minutes

Cooking Time: 15 Minutes

Servings: 3

Ingredients:

- 3 Chicken breasts pieces
- 2 Eggs
- Garlic powder – ½ teaspoon
- Tomato sauce – ½ cup
- Shredded mozzarella – ½ cup
- Breadcrumbs – ¼ cup
- Parmesan cheese – ¼ cup
- Onion powder – ½ teaspoon

- Cooking spray

Instructions:
1. Take a bowl and put eggs.
2. In the 2nd bowl add breadcrumbs, parmesan cheese, onion and garlic powder.
3. Take the chicken pieces and dip egg and then the breadcrumbs mixture.
4. Apply some cooking spray over the basket and place the chicken slices in it.
5. Close the air frying lid and select air crisp mode.
6. Cook for 15 minutes at 360F / 182C.
7. Open the lid and put tomato sauce and sprinkle mozzarella cheese.
8. Cook for another 3 minutes till cheese melts.
9. Take them out and let them cool.
10. After that you can serve it.

Nutritional information per serving: Calories: 463, Fat: 15g, Sodium: 1236mg, Fiber: 2g, Sugar: 5g, Carbohydrate: 14g, Protein: 62g.

17. FRIED CHICKEN WINGS

Preparation Time: 10 Minutes

Cooking Time: 1 Hour

Servings: 3

Ingredients:

- Chicken wings – 2lb / 907g
- Olive oil – 1 tbsp
- Onion powder - ½ teaspoon
- Salt - 2 teaspoon
- Garlic powder - ½ teaspoon

Instructions:

1. Put garlic powder, olive oil, chicken, onion powder, ½ tsp of salt in to a bowl and mix well.
2. Take the rack of your ninja foodi.
3. Keep the chicken wings on the rack.
4. Close the air fryer lid and select air crisp mode.
5. Cook for 25 minutes at 370F / 188C.
6. Switch sides after the first 15 minutes of cooking.
7. Take them out and serve.

Nutritional information per serving: Calories: 410, Fat: 30g, Sodium: 1672mg, Sugar: 1g, Carbohydrate: 2g, Protein: 34g.

18. FRIED PRESSURE COOKED PORK

Preparation Time: 5 Minutes

Cooking Time: 25 Minutes

Servings: 5

Ingredients:

- Pork fillet – 1lb / 454g
- Olive oil – 1 tablespoon
- Paprika – ½ tablespoon
- Cumin – ½ teaspoon
- Black pepper – 1 teaspoon
- Brown sugar - 1 tablespoon
- Chicken broth – ¾ cup
- BBQ sauce – ¾ cup
- Mustard – ½ tablespoon
- Salt – 1 teaspoon

Instructions:

1. Take a bowl and add pepper, salt, paprika, cumin, mustard and brown sugar.
2. In another bowl put chicken broth and bbq sauce. Mix them well.
3. Apply the olive oil on pork slice.
4. Then coat the spices over the pork.
5. Select saute mode in ninja foodi and use high heat.
6. Put pork in to the pot and cook for 3 minutes.
7. Turn the other side and cook the other side.

8. Then include the broth mixture and close the pressure cooking lid.
9. Cook for 10 minutes at high pressure.
10. Serve when the pork reduce the heat.

Nutritional information per serving: Calories: 150, Fat: 18g, Sodium: 938mg, Fiber: 6g, Sugar: 3g, Carbohydrate: 12g, Protein: 27g.

19. GARLIC SEASONED PORK

Preparation Time: 15 Minutes
Cooking Time: 15 Minutes
Servings: 10
Ingredients:
- Minced garlic – 3 tablespoons
- Pork Slice – 2.2lb / 1kg
- Powdered black pepper – 3 teaspoons
- Honey – ¼ cup
- Chili sauce – ¼ cup
- Cornstarch – 2 tablespoons
- Brown sugar - 1 tablespoon
- Chicken broth – 1 cup

Instructions:

1. Take large bowl and put black pepper, garlic and sugar.
2. Mix them well and add pork slice to the mixture and rub the paste over it.
3. Put honey, broth and chili sauce to the cooking pot.
4. Mix them well.
5. Add pork to the pot as well.
6. Close the pressure cooking lid cook for 15 minutes at high pressure.
7. Release the pressure quickly.
8. Remove the pressure lid.
9. Now select saute mode and cook till the liquid reduced.
10. Mix some corn flour to make the gravy thicker.
11. After getting the desired thickness serve the dish.

Nutritional information per serving: Calories: 235, Fat: 36g, Sodium: 1159mg, Fiber: 2g, Sugar: 15g, Carbohydrate: 6g, Protein: 65g.

20. HAM & PEACH ROAST

Preparation Time: 5 Minutes
Cooking Time: 10 Minutes
Servings: 8
Ingredients:

- 1 Cooked ham – 3lbs / 1.36kg
- Chopped peach– 1 cup
- Chili flakes
- Thyme– ¼ teaspoon
- Pepper powder – ¼ teaspoon
- Water – 1 cup

Instructions:

1. Put ham and chopped peaches in to the cooking pot.
2. Close the pressure cooking lid.
3. Pressure cook for 10 minutes in high pressure.
4. Do a quick pressure release. (Check chapter 3).
5. Take a bowl and put chili flakes, thyme and pepper.
6. Mix well and pout over the ham.
7. Close the air fryer lid and select grill function.
8. Use high heat and cook for 10 minutes and serve.

Nutritional information per serving: Calories: 571, Fat: 15g, Sodium: 2876mg, Fiber: 1g, Sugar: 19g, Carbohydrate: 40g, Protein: 68g.

21. HOT & SPICY NUGGETS

Preparation Time: 10 Minutes

Cooking Time: 10 Minutes

Servings: 3

Ingredients:

- Diced chicken wings – 12oz / 340g
- Olive oil – ½ tablespoon
- Cayenne pepper – 1 teaspoon
- Black pepper – ½ teaspoon
- Red pepper flakes – ½ teaspoon
- Brown sugar – 1 tablespoon
- Paprika - 1 teaspoon
- Chili powder - 1 teaspoon
- Garlic powder – ½ teaspoon

Instructions:

1. Put all the ingredients to a bowl and mix well.
2. Add oil and further mix them.
3. Move the mixture to the basket and close the air fryer lid.
4. Select air crisp mode.
5. Cook for 10 minutes at 400F / 204C.
6. Serve after it is cool enough.

Nutritional information per serving: Calories: 130, Fat: 4g, Sodium: 453mg, Fiber: 1g, Sugar: 23g, Carbohydrate: 1g, Protein: 25g.

22. PORK CHOPS & SOUR CREAM

Preparation Time: 10 Minutes
Cooking Time: 20 Minutes
Servings: 4
Ingredients:

- Coconut oil – 1 tbsp
- Sliced onions
- Chili sauce – 1 tsp
- Cornstarch– 1tsp
- Sour cream – 1/3 cup
- 4 Pork chops
- Salt & pepper

- Water – 1 cup

Instructions:
1. Select saute mode in the ninja foodi.
2. Put butter and onion till they become tender.
3. Add Pork, salt, oil, water and pepper as well.
4. Stop the saute mode and add chili sauce and mix.
5. Close the pressure cooking lid and cook for 8 minutes in high pressure.
6. Quick release the pressure and add corn flour to increase the thickness of the liquid.
7. Serve with sour cream.

Nutritional information per serving: Calories: 304, Fat: 15g, Sodium: 253mg, Fiber: 2g, Sugar: 2g, Carbohydrate: 7g, Protein: 31g.

23. PRESSURE COOKED BACK RIBS

Preparation Time: 15 Minutes
Cooking Time: 45 Minutes
Servings: 5
Ingredients:
- Beef ribs – 2lbs / 907g
- Salt – 1½ teaspoon
- Beef broth – ¼ cup
- Sugar – 2 tablespoons

- Minced garlic – 2 tablespoons
- Thyme – 1 tablespoon
- Minced ginger – ½ tablespoon
- Pepper – 1 teaspoon
- Olive oil – 3 tablespoons
- 1 Diced onion

Instructions:

1. Put olive to the cooking pot and select saute mode.
2. Season ribs with salt and pepper in a bowl.
3. Add the broth to the pot.
4. Include garlic, onions in to the pot.
5. Add ginger, thyme and sugar to the pot.
6. Close the pressure cooking lid and cook for 40 minutes at medium pressure.
7. Do a quick pressure release and open the lid.
8. Put some corn flour and mix to increase the thickness of the liquid and serve.

Nutritional information per serving: Calories: 437, Fat: 28g, Sodium: 1038mg, Fiber: 1g, Sugar: 5g, Carbohydrate: 12g, Protein: 31g.

24. PORK TORTILLAS

Preparation Time: 15 Minutes

Cooking Time: 45 Minutes

Servings: 10

Ingredients:

- Pork – 1lbs / 454g
- Olive oil spray
- Chopped garlic – 1 clove
- ½ Lemon juice
- Chili powder – ½ teaspoon
- Cooked tortillas
- Oregano - ½ teaspoon
- Cumin - ½ teaspoon

- Sliced red pepper
- Water – ½ cup
- Salt - ¼ teaspoon
- Pepper - ¼ teaspoon
- Diced onion, – ¼ cup

Instructions:
1. Put olive oil in to the pot.
2. Cut pork in to small slices.
3. Put in the cooking pot and cook in saute mode till it gets fried.
4. Add water, lemon juice, salt, onion, garlic, pepper, oregano, cumin, chili powder and chopped bell pepper in to the pot.
5. Mix well and close the pressure cooking lid and cook for 35 minutes at high pressure.
6. Let pressure release naturally. (Leave 20 minutes. Do nothing)
7. Open the pressure valve before open the lid.
8. Take the pork out and serve with tortillas.

Nutritional information per serving: Calories: 497, Fat: 35g, Sodium: 186mg, Fiber: 1g, Sugar: 2g, Carbohydrate: 4g, Protein: 38g.

25. PORK SALSA

Preparation Time: 20 Minutes
Cooking Time: 20 Minutes
Servings: 12
Ingredients:

- 2 Pork fillets
- Olive Oil – 2 tablespoons
- Garlic – 4 cloves
- Paprika – 1 teaspoon
- Salt – 1 teaspoon
- Lemon juice - 2 tablespoons
- Soy sauce - 2 tablespoons
- Water – 1 cup
- ½ an onion
- 2 Seeded jalapeno peppers

Instructions:

1. Put olive oil, onion, jalapeno, garlic and soy sauce to a bowl and mix well.
2. Put in a blender and get a smooth mixture.
3. Add salt, paprika and pork to the cooking pot.
4. Put the ninja foodi in to saute high mode and fry the pork well.
5. Stop the saute mode and add soy sauce, water and lemon juice mix and close the pressure cooking lid.
6. Cook for 15 minute at high pressure.

7. Release pressure quickly and open the lid.
8. Select grill function and cook till the liquid evaporates.
9. Then serve the pork fillets.

Nutritional information per serving: Calories: 136, Fat: 15g, Sodium: 53mg, Carbohydrate: 1g, Protein: 23g.

26. ROASTED BRISKET

Preparation Time: 10 Minutes
Cooking Time: 1 Hour
Servings: 12
Ingredients:

- Brisket – 3lbs / 1.36kg
- Water – ½ cup
- Olive oil
- BBQ Sauce – ½ cup

Instructions:
1. Put olive oil in to the pot.
2. Add beef slice and cook both sides under saute mode. Use high heat.
3. Add water in to the pot.
4. Close pressure lid and cook for 20 minutes at high heat.
5. Quick release the pressure. (Refer chapter 3).
6. Open the lid and take the brisket out.

7. Discard the liquid.
8. Place the brisket on the rack and apply bbq sauce on both sides.
9. Select air crisp mode and close the air fryer lid.
10. Cook for 15 minutes at 380F / 193C.
11. Switch sides after 7 minutes.
12. When it is done, let it cool and serve.

Nutritional information per serving: Calories: 471, Fat: 30g, Sodium: 269mg, Sugar: 4g, Carbohydrate: 5g, Protein: 45g.

27. STUFFED CHICKEN

Preparation Time: 10 Minutes
Cooking Time: 12 Minutes
Servings: 4
Ingredients:

- 4 Chicken thighs (without bones)
- Green beans – 1 can
- Chicken stock – 1 cup
- Chicken seasoning – 1 pack
- Water – 1½ cups
- Olive oil spray

Instructions:

1. Put 1 water cup to the pot.
2. Take the baking pan and spray oil over it.

3. Add the chicken in to the pan.
4. Put chicken seasoning and water over it.
5. Include green beans and chicken stock.
6. Close the pressure lid and cook for 12 minutes in high pressure.
7. Quick release the pressure.
8. Serve the meal.

Nutritional information per serving: Calories: 457, Fat: 18g, Sodium: 787mg, Fiber: 5g, Sugar: 4g, Carbohydrate: 24g, Protein: 54g.

28. SPICY FRIED HAM

Preparation Time: 10 Minutes

Cooking Time: 5 Minutes

Servings: 10

Ingredients:

- Ham – 5lbs / 2.26kg
- Water – 1/3 cup
- Cornstarch – 4 tablespoons
- Brown sugar – 1 cup
- Honey – ¼ cup
- 3 Whole cloves

Instructions:

1. Put sugar in to the cooking pot.

2. Add water as well.
3. Include ham to the pot and mix well with sugar.
4. Add whole cloves to the pot.
5. Close the pressure cooking lid.
6. Cook for 5 minutes in high pressure.
7. Naturally release the pressure. (10 minutes)
8. Open pressure valve prior to open the lid.
9. Add corn flour to the pot to gain the required thickness.
10. Serve the ham.

Nutritional information per serving: Calories: 675, Fat: 37g, Sodium: 2698mg, Fiber: 1g, Sugar: 24g, Carbohydrate: 32g, Protein: 52g.

29. SWEET FRIED CHICKEN

Preparation Time: 5 Minutes

Cooking Time: 30 Minutes

Servings: 4

Ingredients:

- 4 Chicken Drumsticks
- Maple syrup – ½ cup
- Cinnamon powder
- 2 Sliced sweet potatoes
- Cooking spray

Instructions:

1. Apply cooking spray over the cooking pot.
2. Put sweet potatoes in to pot.

3. Place the rack inside the pot and put drumsticks on it.
4. Run cinnamon powder and maple syrup over it.
5. Close the air fryer lid and select air crisp mode.
6. Then cook for 25 minutes at 390F / 198C.
7. Once it is done take everything out and mix in a dish and serve.

Nutritional information per serving: Calories: 918, Fat: 35g, Sodium: 405mg, Fiber: 5g, Sugar: 30g, Carbohydrate: 53g, Protein: 95g.

30. TENDER CHICKEN FRIES

Preparation Time: 10 Minutes

Cooking Time: 15 Minutes

Servings: 4

Ingredients:

- Chicken tenders – 1lb / 454g
- Pepper powder – ½ teaspoon
- Garlic powder – ½ teaspoon
- 3 Eggs
- Flour – ½ cup
- Breadcrumbs – ½ cup
- Parmesan cheese – ¼ cup

- Salt – ½ teaspoon
- Tomato sauce

Instructions:

1. Take a bowl and mix cheese, breadcrumbs, pepper, salt and garlic powder.
2. Put mixed eggs to another bowl.
3. Add flout to another bowl.
4. Take chicken tender and dip in flour, egg and breadcrumb bowls.
5. Place them in the basket and close the air fryer lid of ninja foodi.
6. Select air crisp mode and cook for 8 minutes at 400F / 204C.
7. Take them out and serve with tomato sauce.

Nutritional information per serving: Calories: 296, Fat: 5g, Sodium: 634mg, Fiber: 1g, Sugar: 2g, Carbohydrate: 18g, Protein: 35g.

CONCLUSION

Through recent years manufactures have developed multi cookers in to cutting edge standards. Due to that there is a huge demand for multi cookers in current market. The main reason for that is the efficiency. You can almost cook any type of food in your multi cooker. When it comes to ninja foodi multi cookers, there are several added advantages. The main difference is the air frying capability. With the air fryer lid several other functionalities have been included in this equipment. Such as grill and broil. The other main important fact of ninja foodi multi cooker is the "tender crisp technology". That technology was founded by ninja foodi. It will help you o make your food tender as well as crispier. Combination of air fryer and pressure cooker will help you to gain that result.

That was just a one benefit you can have from the ninja foodi multi cooker. You can see several reasons on how this product can improve your lifestyle and so on. The most important reason is the practicality. This appliance fits perfectly well with our busy life style. Most of the time people want efficient solutions. But there are very limited number of kitchen appliances which offers efficient and healthy outcomes. That is where ninja foodi multi cooker beats the rest. This is efficient as well as healthy appliance. For an example I would like to mention about the air frying function. You don't have to use lot of oil to use this option. Only a little amount of oil will be needed to cook an entire dish. Sometimes you will be able cook from the inbuilt oil of the food item. That is something you won't get in other products.

There are many guides and books related to this product. But it is really difficult to find a book which has all the relevant information regarding this product. This book has answered all those questions. Even a new user can gain a lot of knowledge by referring this book. Not only for them but also for an experienced use also this book can give a new perspective. Because some of them might have used this product in a wrong way. Or else they might not have had the proper guidance about using this equipment. From chapter one to chapter to chapter six everything you should know regarding the ninja foodi multi cooker have been mentioned in detail.

Those chapters include setup guide, controlling, different modes, cleaning, maintenance, things to avoid and the advantages user can benefit have described in details with examples. I would like to suggest you to read all the chapters carefully. Because these first chapters are so important for any ninja foodi multi cooker user. After that you will get to know the recipes that you can try from your ninja foodi multi cooker. Recipes have been categorized under seven categories. So you can try them according to the requirement. All the types of meals have been included in the recipes. So you can try them under you preference. They are healthy as well as delicious. So this book has succeeded on addressing the targeted audience of ninja foodi multi cooker in every aspect. Has covered every corner.

"Really appreciate if you could express your experience of this book in a review. Because it will help other readers to find this book. That is a great favour for me as an author. Thank you."

Printed in Great Britain
by Amazon